# The Garden

Fred Biggar

Mud Road
2024

FIRST EDITION

"Il faut cultiver notre jardin."

-Voltaire, *Candide*

Isolation. Day Seven. If there was someone to write to, what remains to say? Grading, and the dishes done. I can do twenty-five push ups in a row. The green tea from the back of the cupboard tastes like straw. I smell like a horse. Folks I haven't spoken to in years soon find time to

So I have opened the windows as far as they can go. Sweat out the afternoon. Dust gathers on the desk and coats the palm trees in the courtyard below. Mosquitos and street dogs. Raptors and

pigeons move about freely. Unseen leopards wait for better light. The anxious crowd the television, relieved there was something to be worried about all along, debate the businessmen who want us to die for the economy. I miss the abstraction of a

A pile of things to burn or bury remains. Each word I've ever written tipped into a dumpster behind the building, or into an open sewer that flows from Goregaon to the sea. A window that won't open wide enough to allow for any impact.

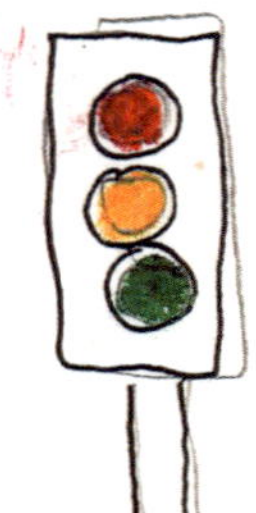

## Mumbai - Prelude

Isolation. Day seven. If there was home to write to, what remains to say? Grading and the dishes done. I can do twenty-five pushups in a row. The green tea from the back of the cupboard tastes like straw and I smell like a horse. Folks I haven't spoken to in years now find time to—

So I have opened the windows as far as they can go, sweat out the afternoon. Dirt gathers on the desk and coats the palm trees in the courtyard below. Mosquitoes and street dogs. Raptors and—

Pigeons move about freely. Unseen, leopards wait for better light. The anxious crowd the television, relieved there was something to be worried about all along, they debate the businessmen who wants us to die for the economy. I miss the abstraction of a—

A pile of things to burn or bury remains. Each word I've ever written tipped into a dumpster behind the building. Or into an open sewer that flows from Goregaon to the sea. A window that won't open wide enough to allow for any impact.

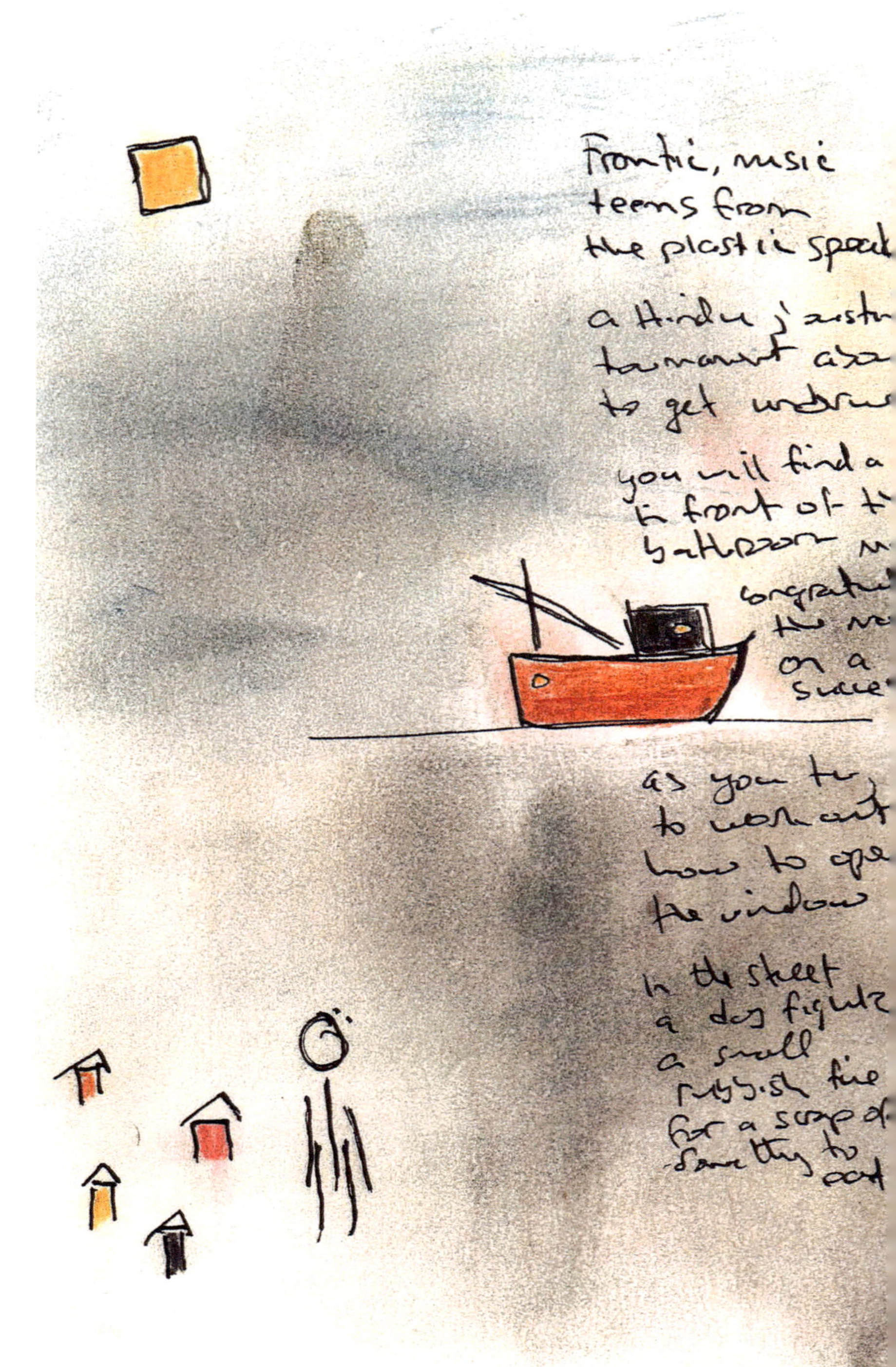
Frantic, music
teems from
the plastic speak
a Hindu
to get
you will find a
in front of
bathroom
on a
as you try
to work out
how to ope
the window
in the street
a dog fights
a small
rubbish fire
for a scrap o
something to

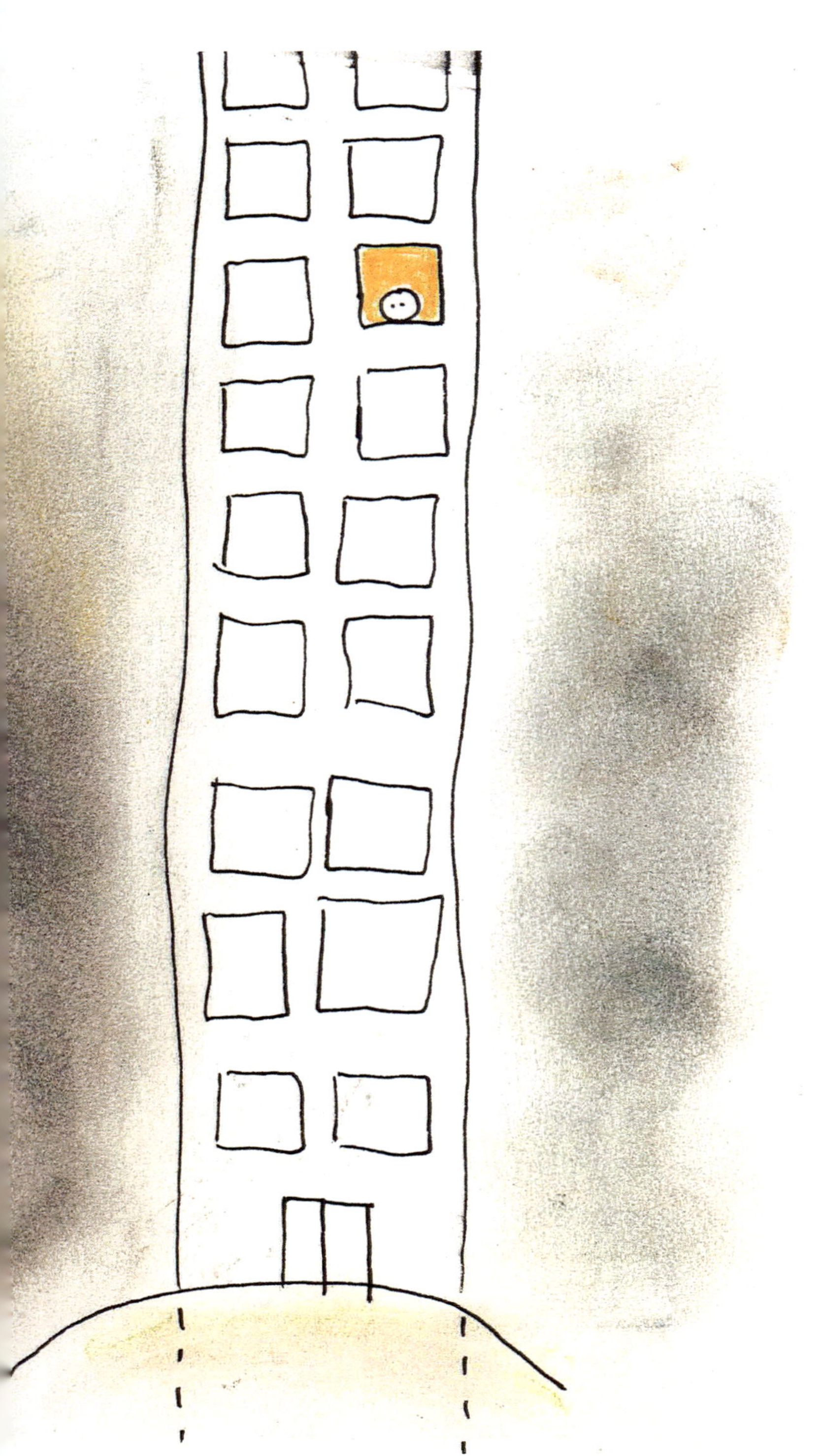

## Antananarivo

Is there a story that I have been meaning to tell? An idea I want to share or a point I need to prove? Is it foolish to argue that there is no point in arguing a point of view? As if two eyes could ever occupy the same...

Field poems, but furrows of text designed only to fill up the blank spaces between words on a piece of paper. Letters as seed an so on. Finish the conceit for homework. Lorem ipsum est, motherfucker, long gone the loquitor. I think I've said something along these lines before.

The guard checks the gate for the fourth time in the last thirty minutes or half hour if you prefer fractions to intgers. This morning the water was off so the clothes are still on the line.

Later on, when it gets dark out here in the garden, you'll hear a lot fewer birds but the flowers will begin to tell stories, and the street lights.

Without glasses it's hard to see what I have put down.

Most days the dead flowers in the gutter

Many days
the colorful petals in the ditch
are not enough

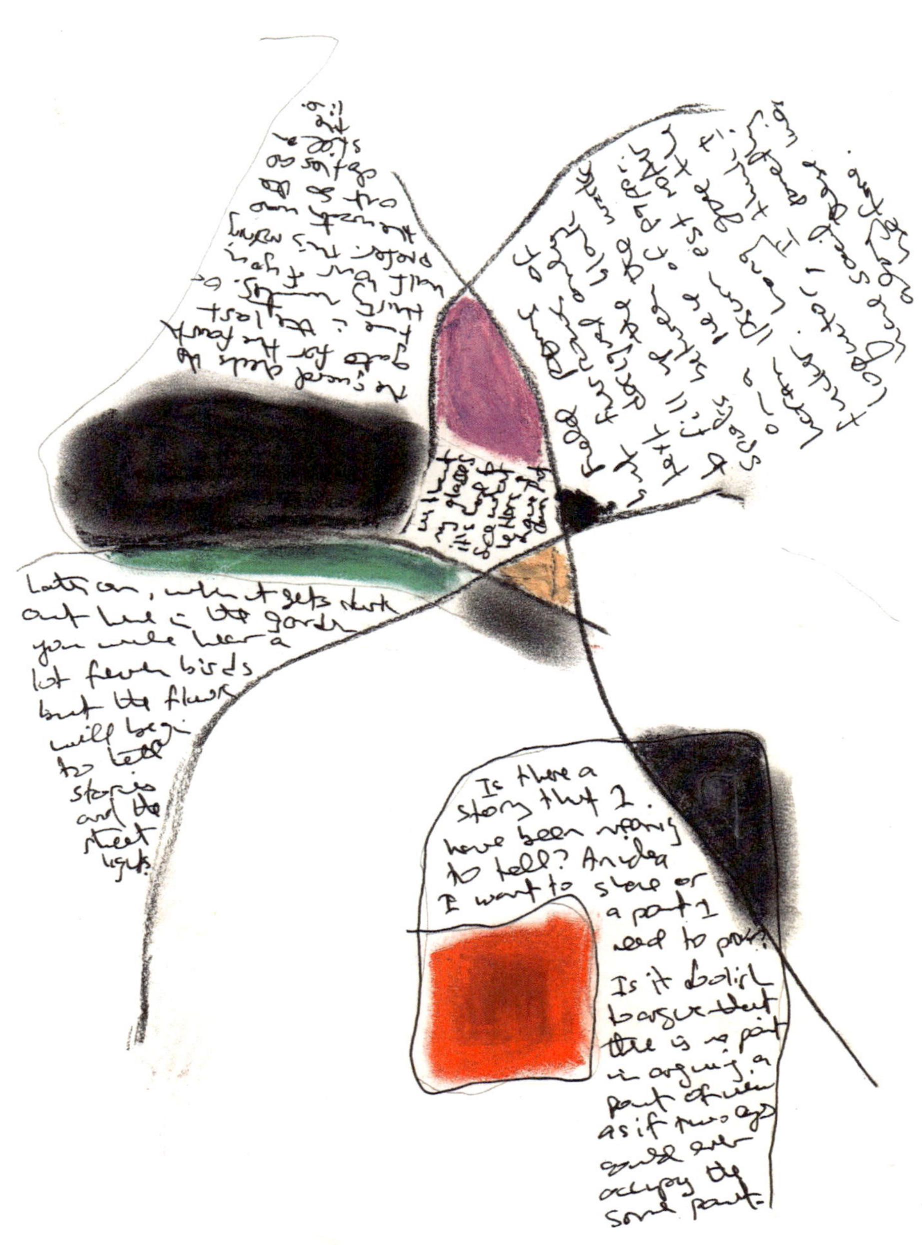
Later on, when it gets dark
out here in the garden
you will hear a
lot fewer birds
but the flowers
will begin
to tell
stories
and the
street
lights.
Is there a
story that I
have been wanting
to tell? And do
I want to share or
a point I
need to push?
Is it foolish
to argue that
there is no point
in arguing a
point of view
as if two egos
could ever
occupy the
same point.

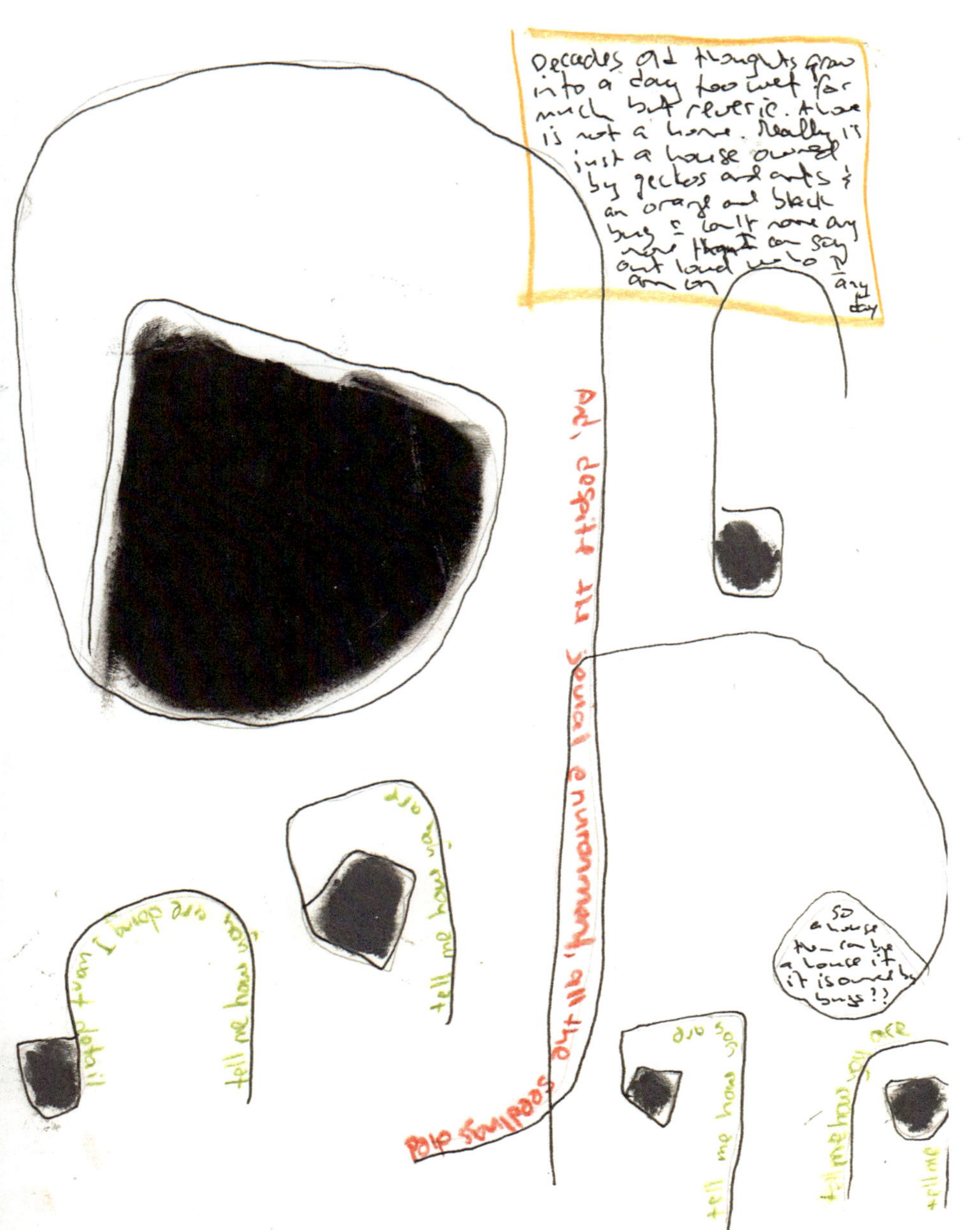
Decades old thoughts grow into a day too wet for much but reverie. A home is not a home. Really it's just a house owned by geckos and ants & an orange and black bug I can't name any more than I can say out loud who I am on any day
And, despite the social environment, all the goodness olds
tell me how you are doing I want detail
tell me how you are
tell me how you are
tell me how you are
tell me
So a house then can be a house if it is owned by bugs??

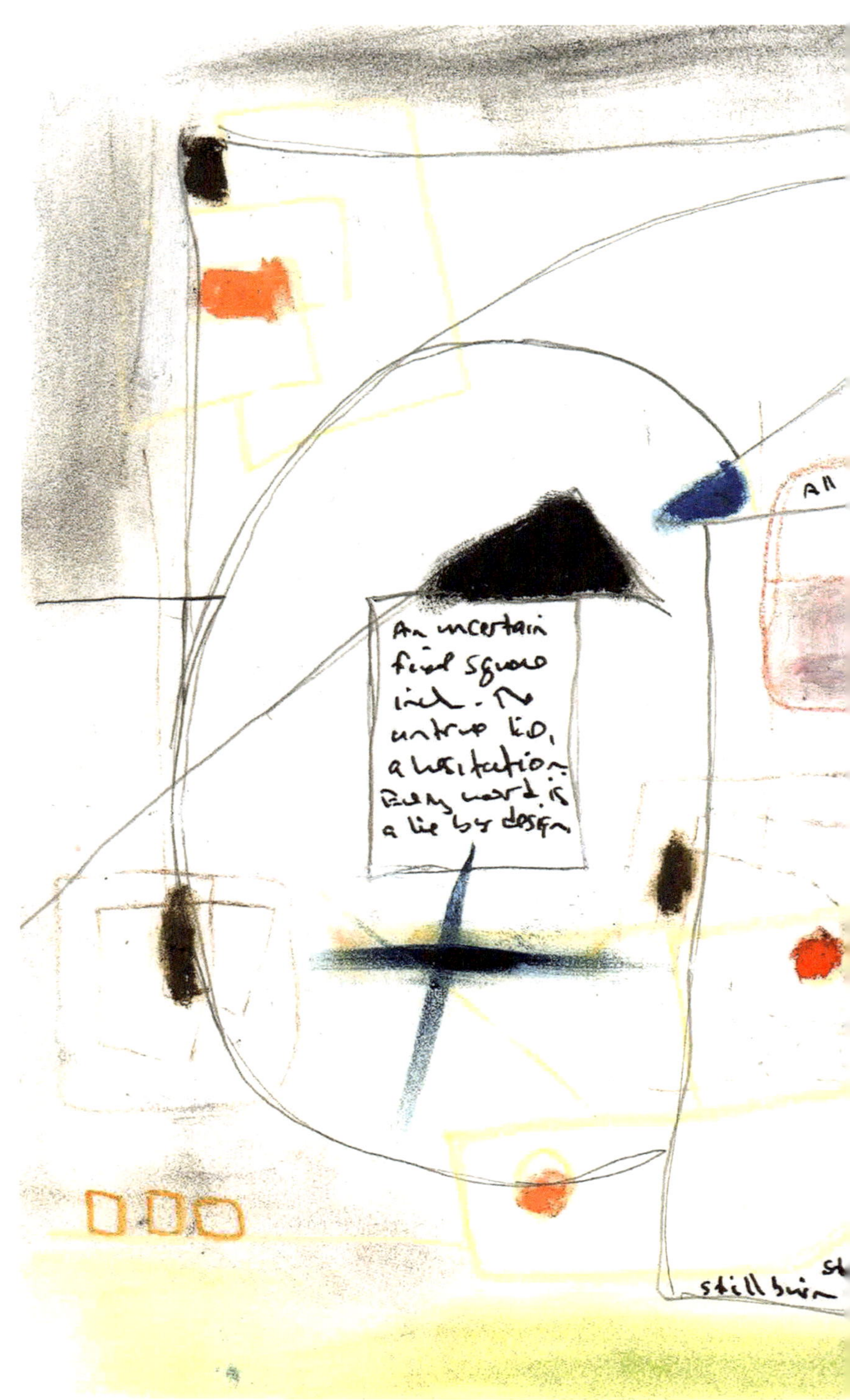
An uncertain
first square
inch. No
untrue lie,
a hesitation.
Every word is
a lie by design
All
still born

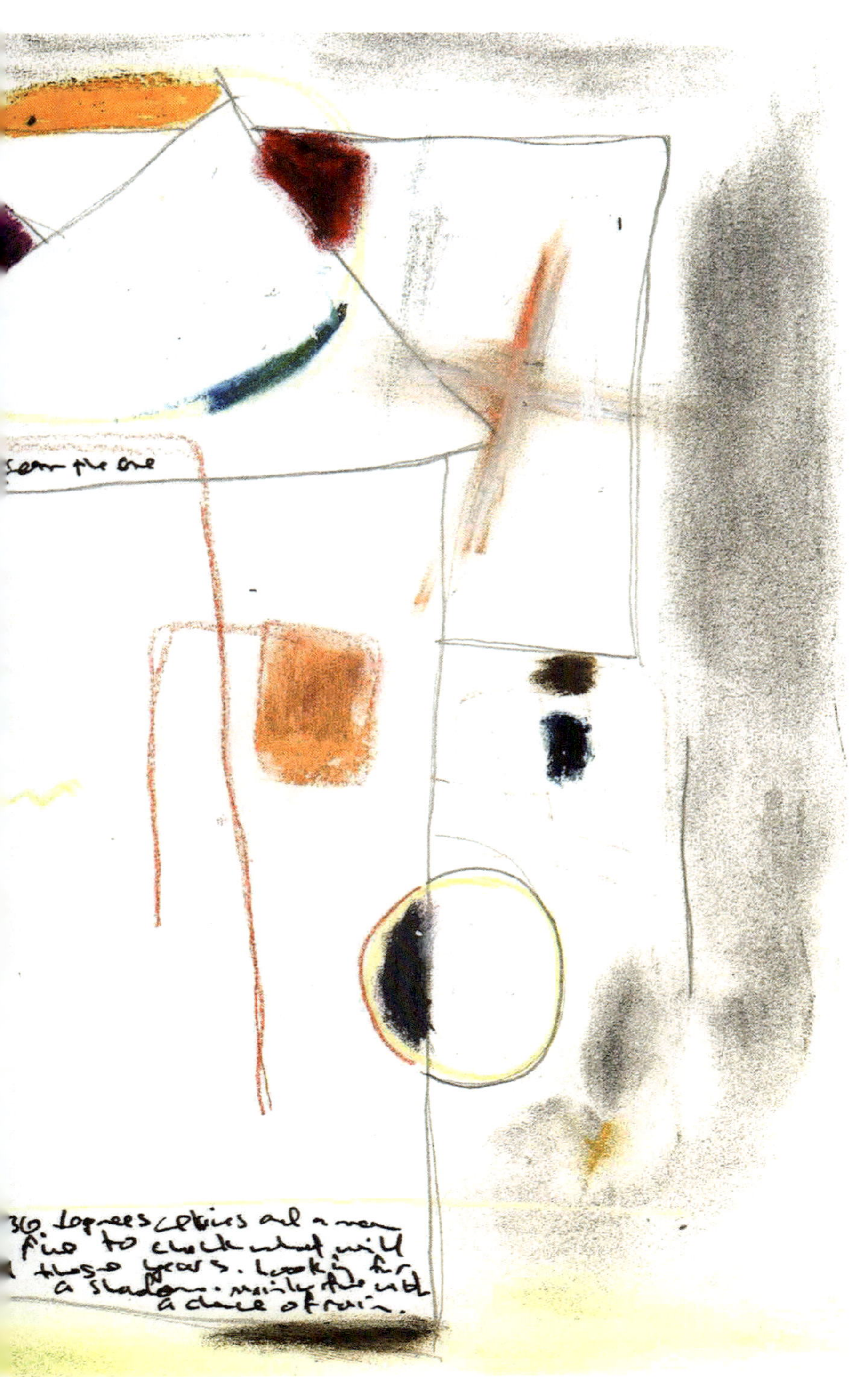
36 degrees celsius and a new
fire to check what will
these years. Looking for
a shadow. mainly fine with
a chance of rain.

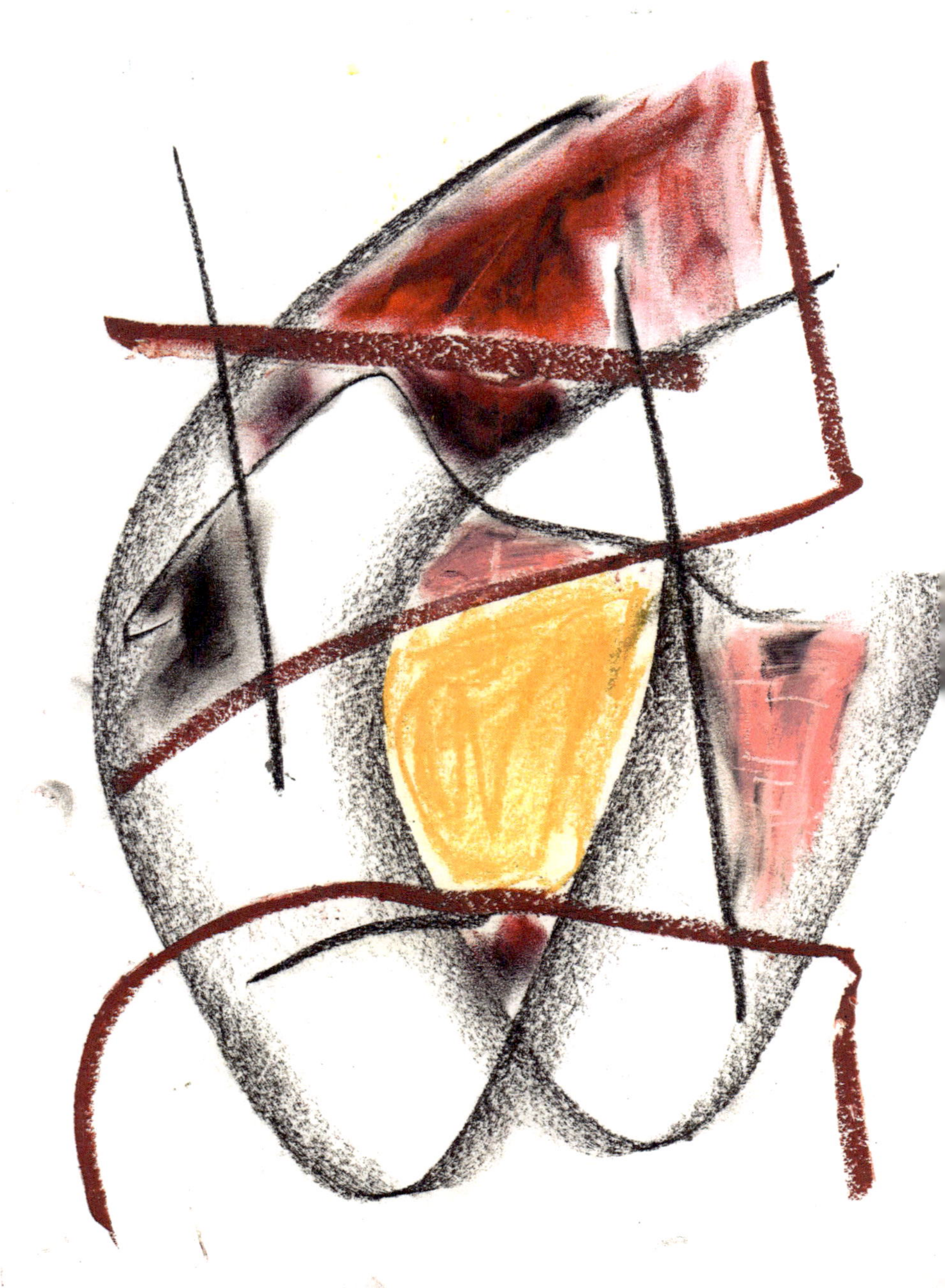

## Mainly fine with a chance of rain.

July 1st.
36 degrees Celsius
and a man will still set a fire
looking for shadows,

to see what will
burn after all these years.

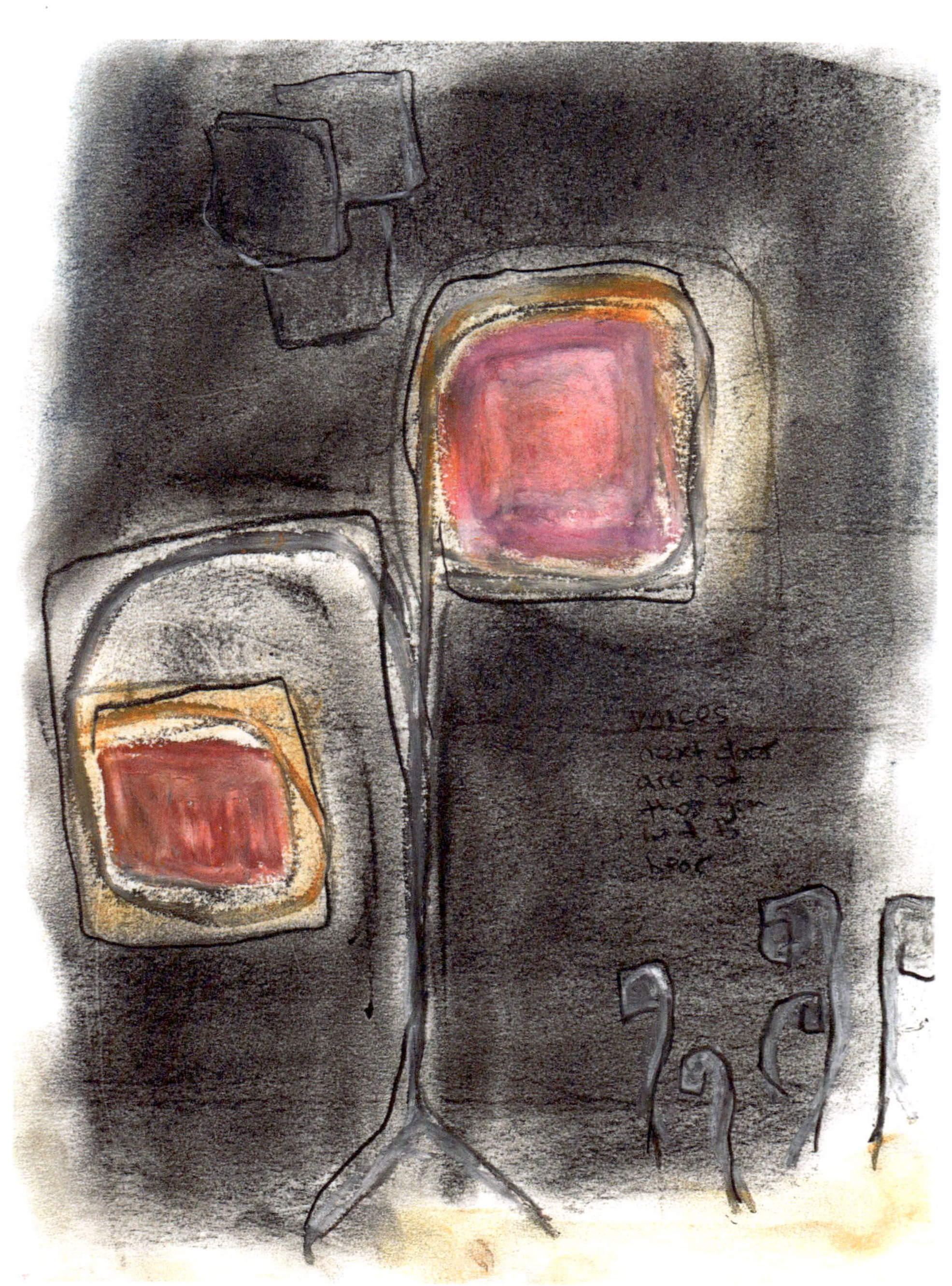
voices
next door
are not
those you
hear

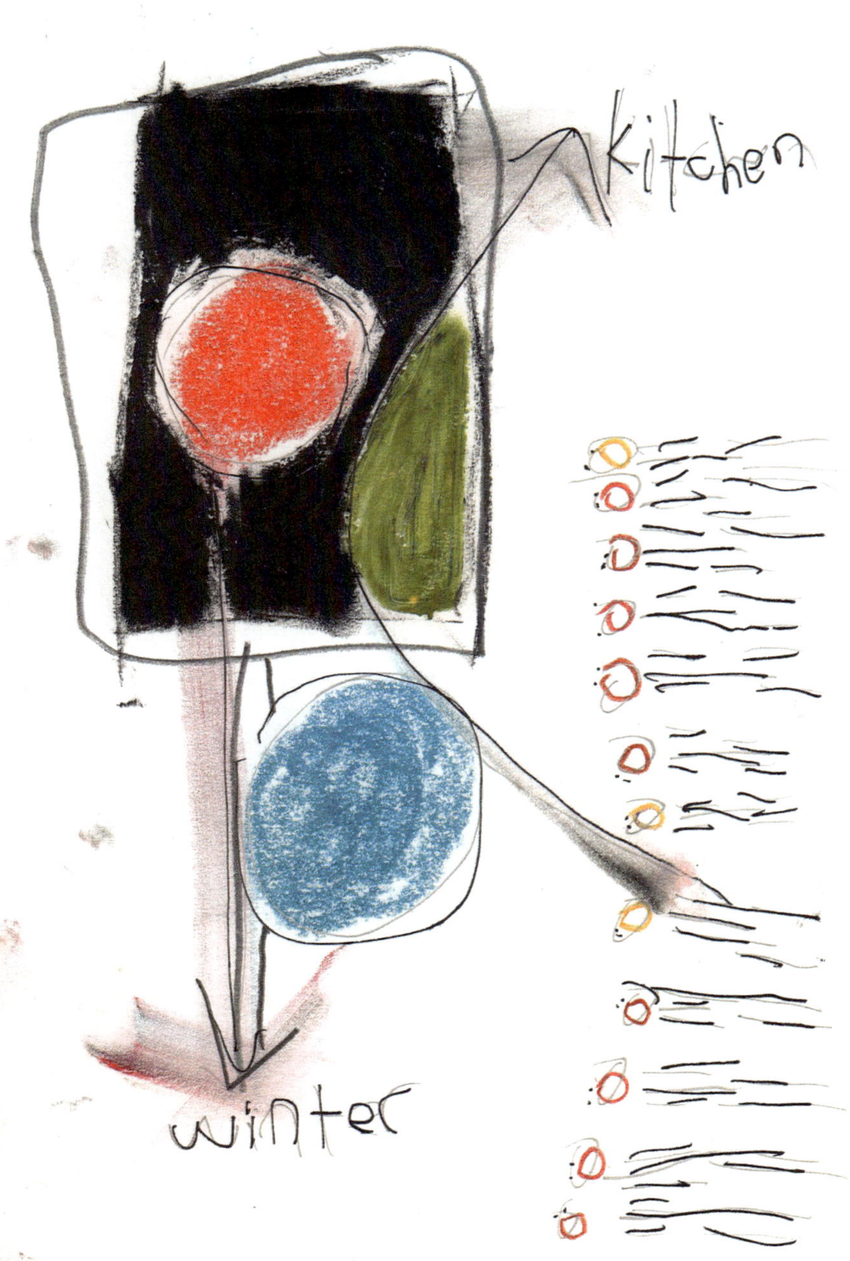
Kitchen
winter

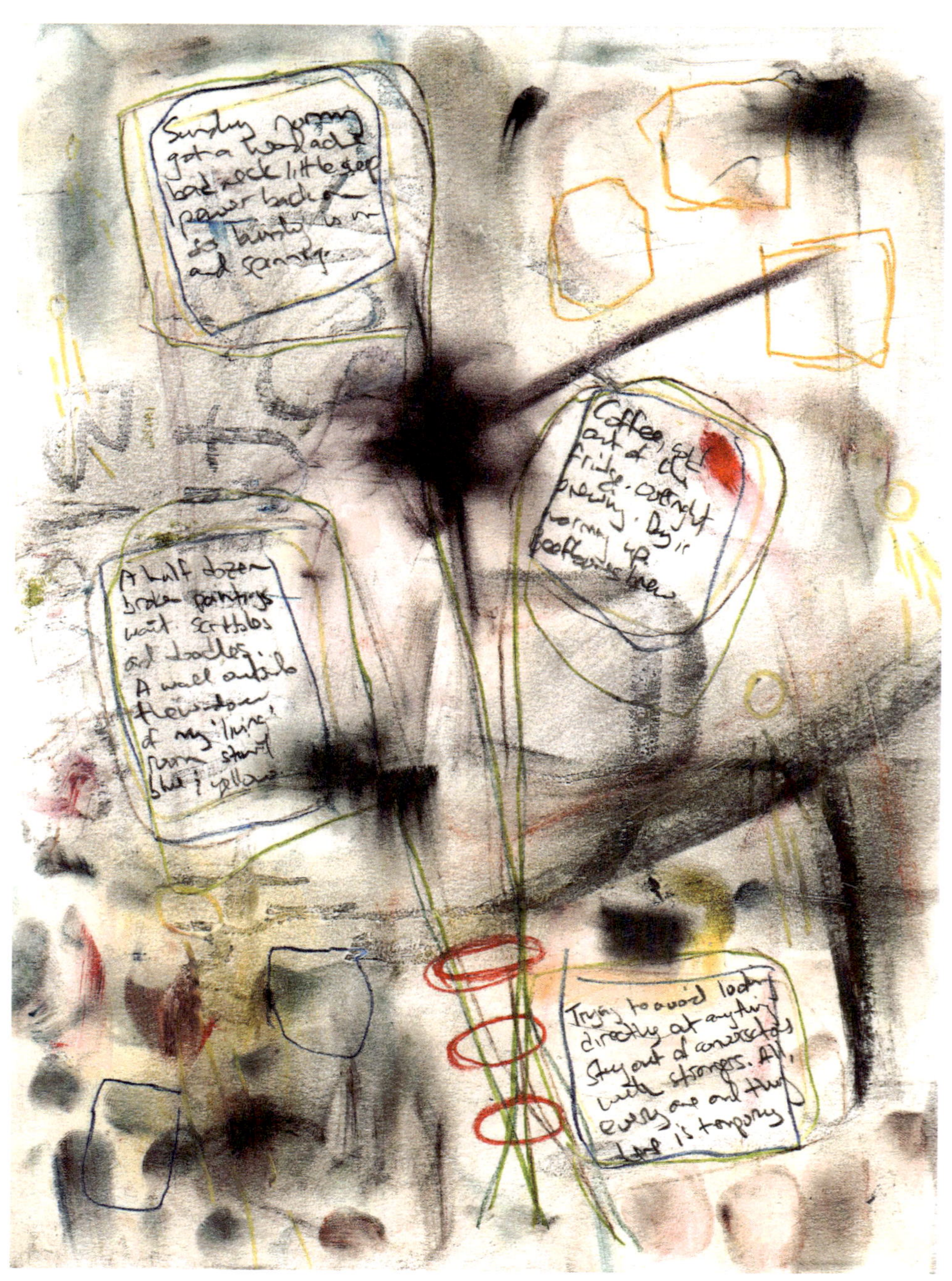
Sunday morning
got a headache
bad neck little sleep
power back on
A half dozen
broken paintings
wait. scribbles
and doodles.
A wall outside
the window
of my 'living'
room stained
blue & yellow
Coffee,
out of the
fridge. overnight
brewing. Day is
warming up.
Trying to avoid looking
directly at anything
Stay out of conversations
with strangers. All,
everyone and thing
is temporary

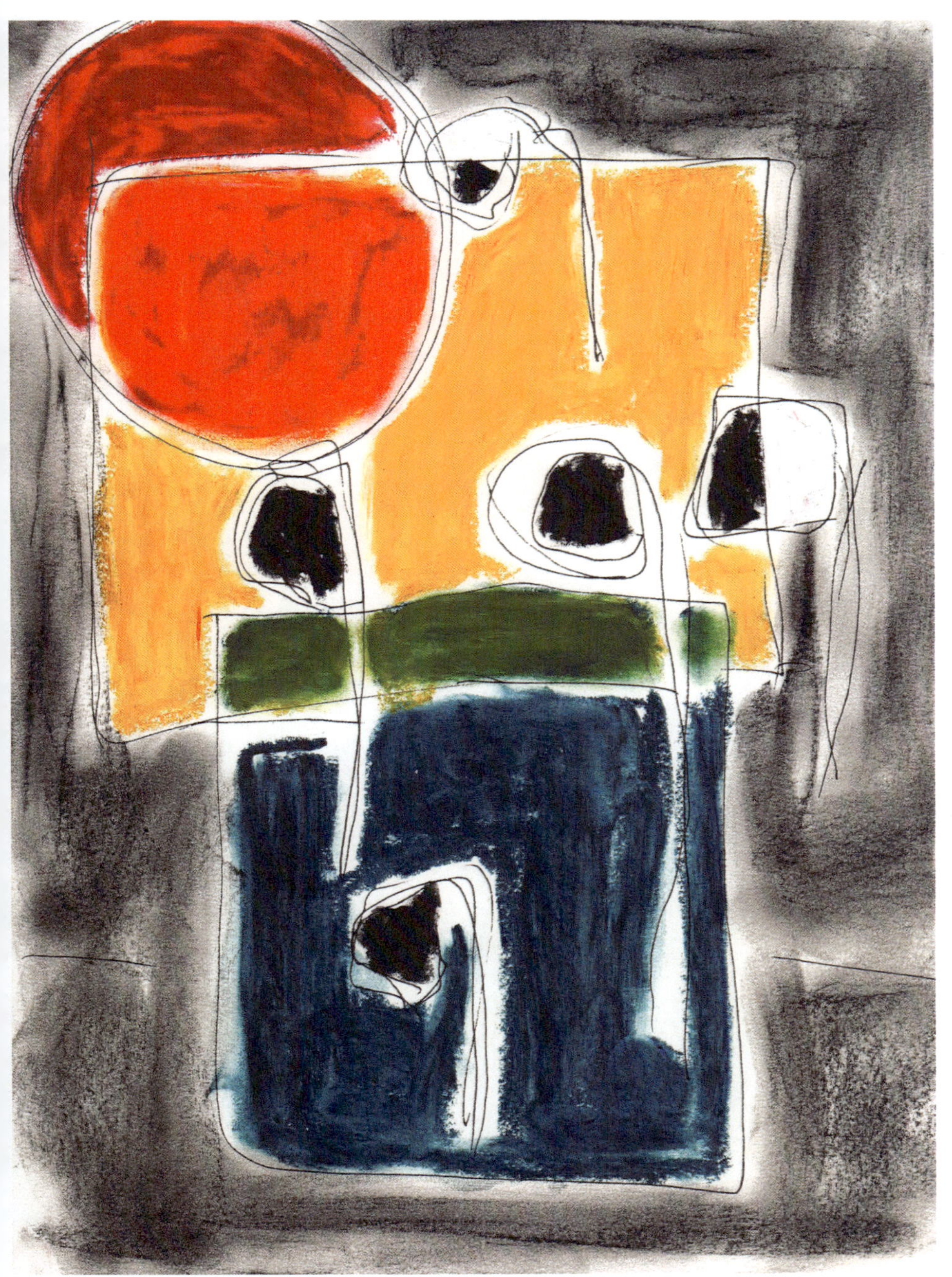

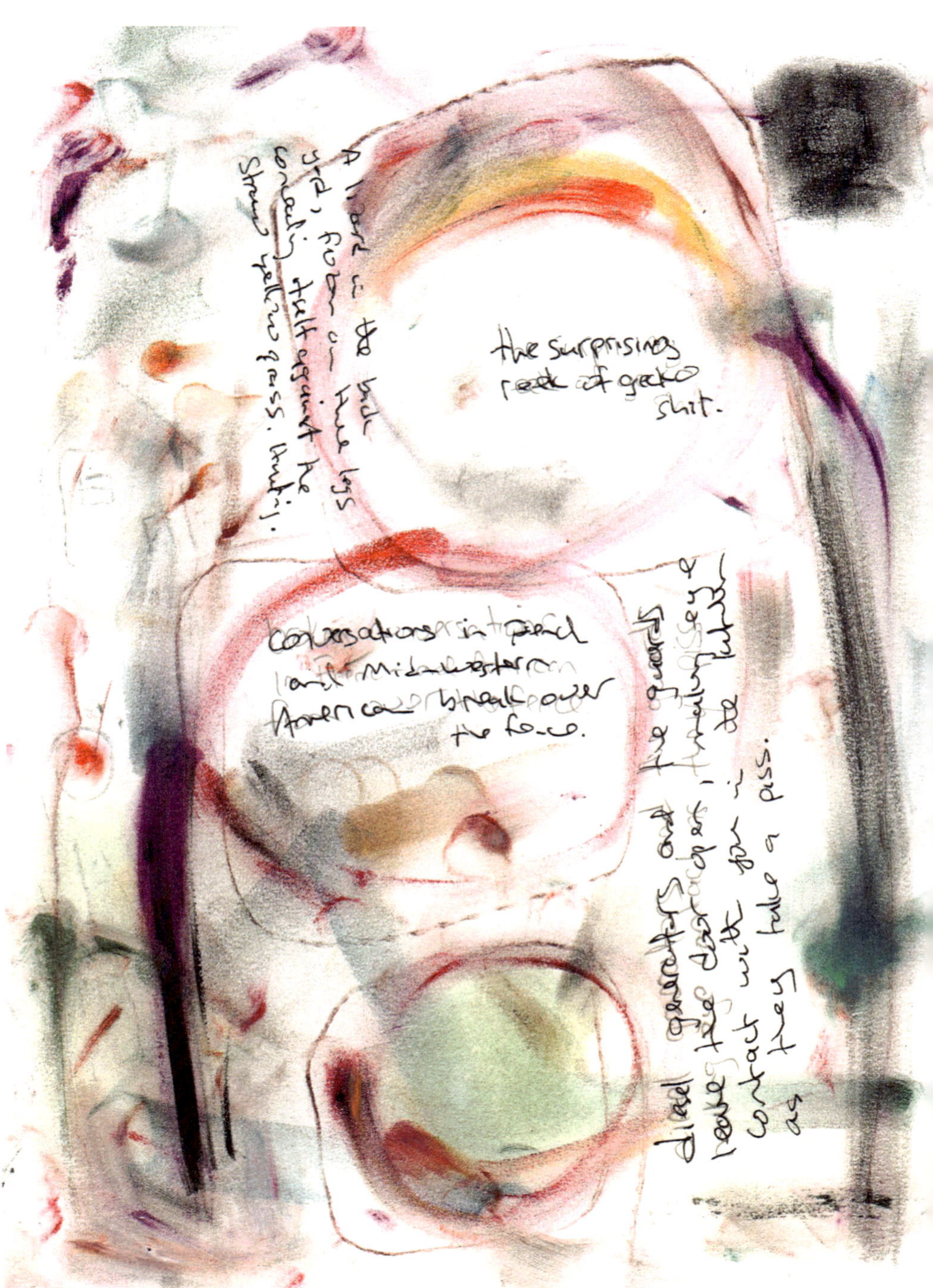
the surprising reek of gecko shit.
A lizard in the back yard, frozen on three legs concealing itself against the straw yellow grass. Waiting.
conversations in typical Midwestern American break over the fence.
diesel generators and the guards
as they take a piss.

## All the blues seem the same to him.

A hazy
final square
inch. The
untrue line,

a hesitation.

Each and every word a lie by design.

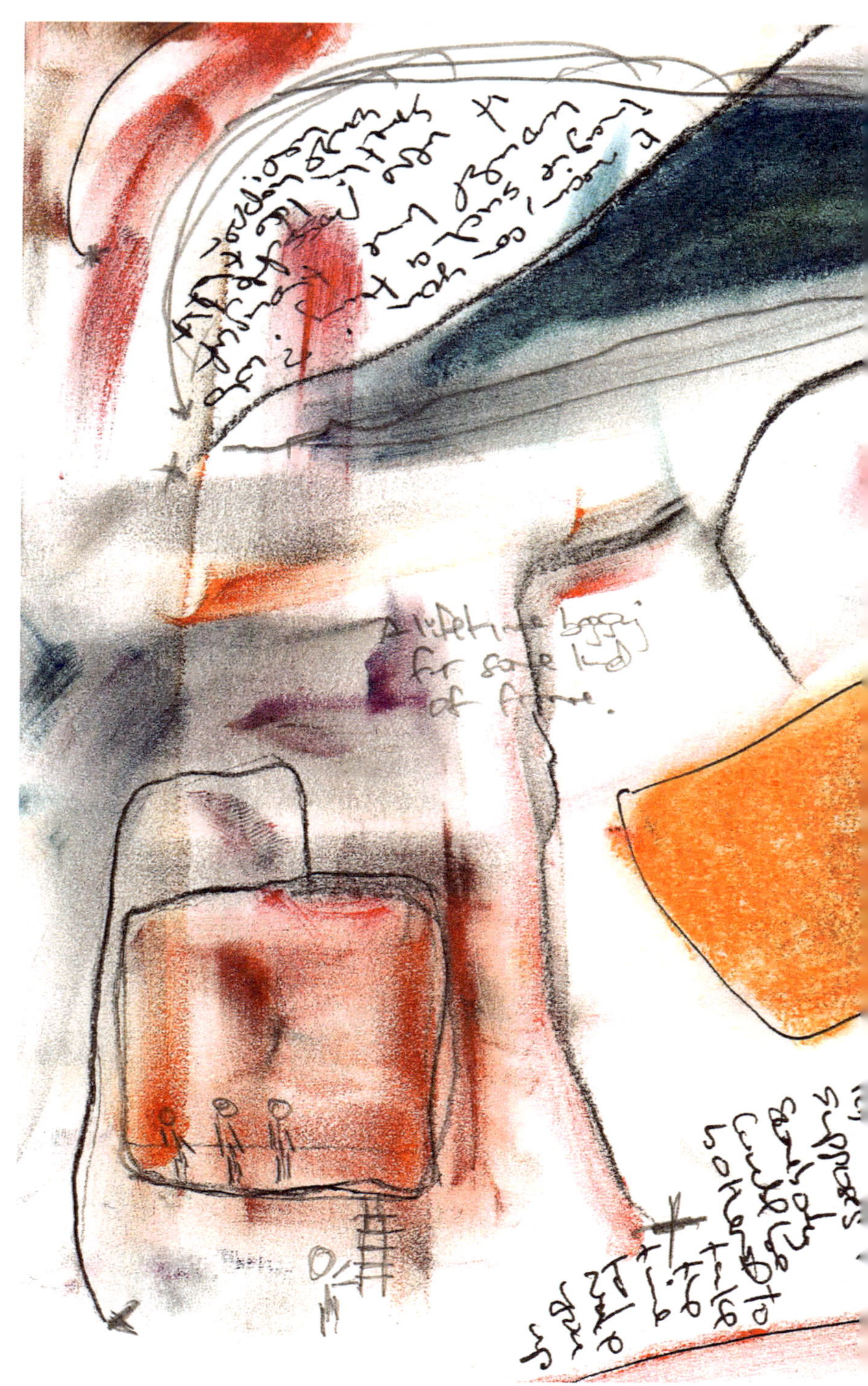

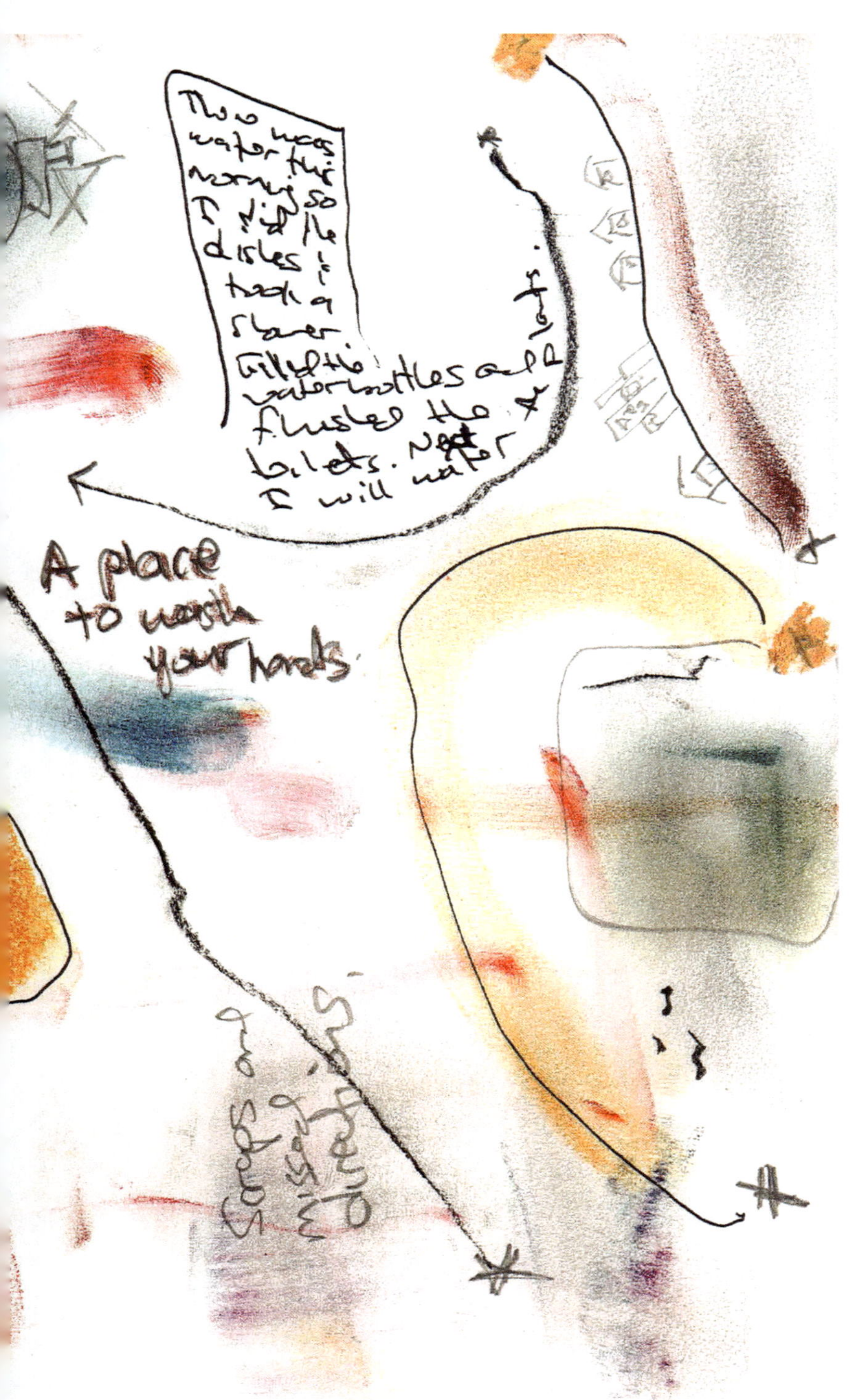
There was water this morning so I did the dishes & took a shower filled the water bottles and flushed the toilets. Next I will water plants.
A place to wash your hands
Scraps and missing directions

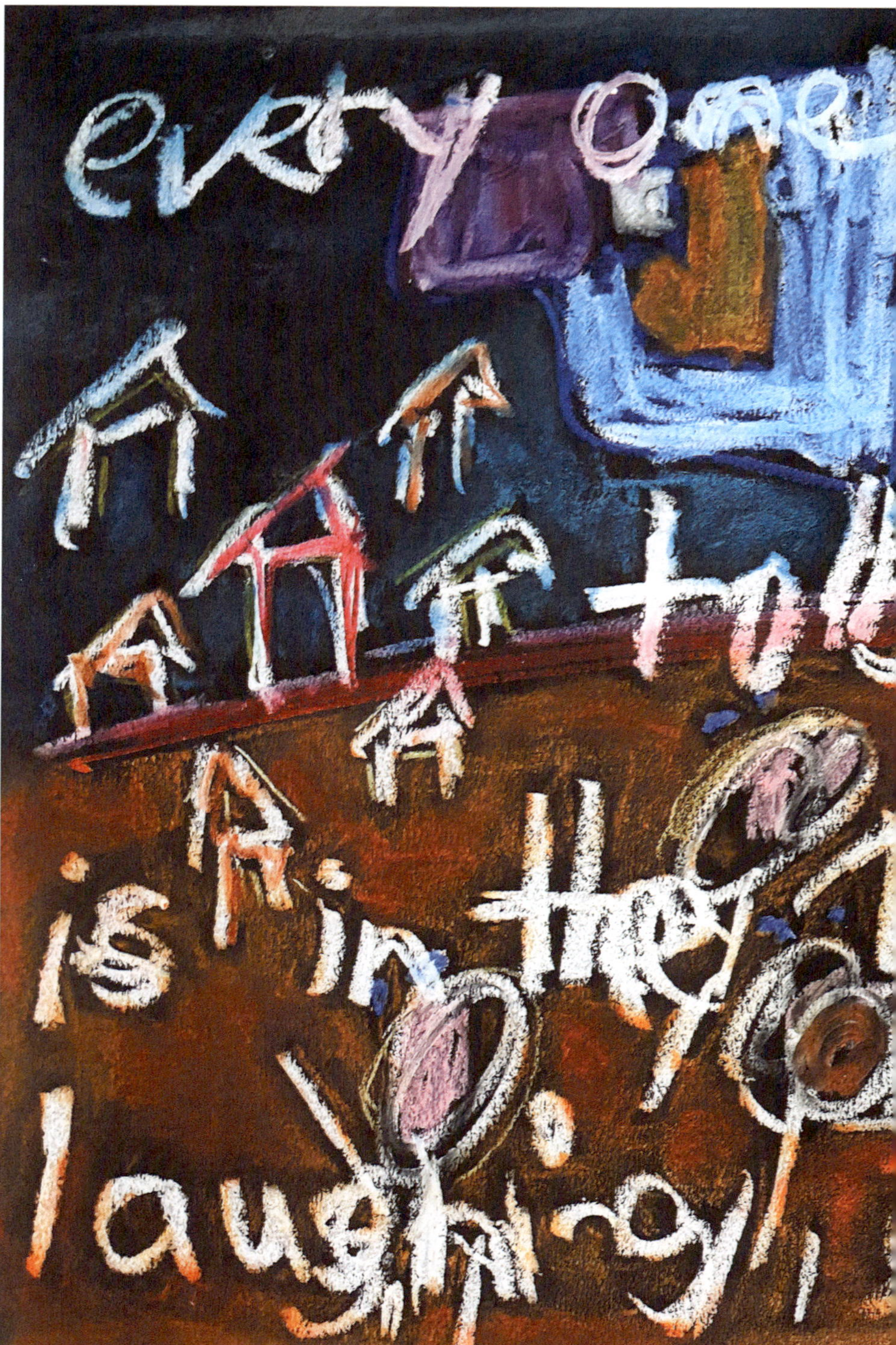
is in the
laughing

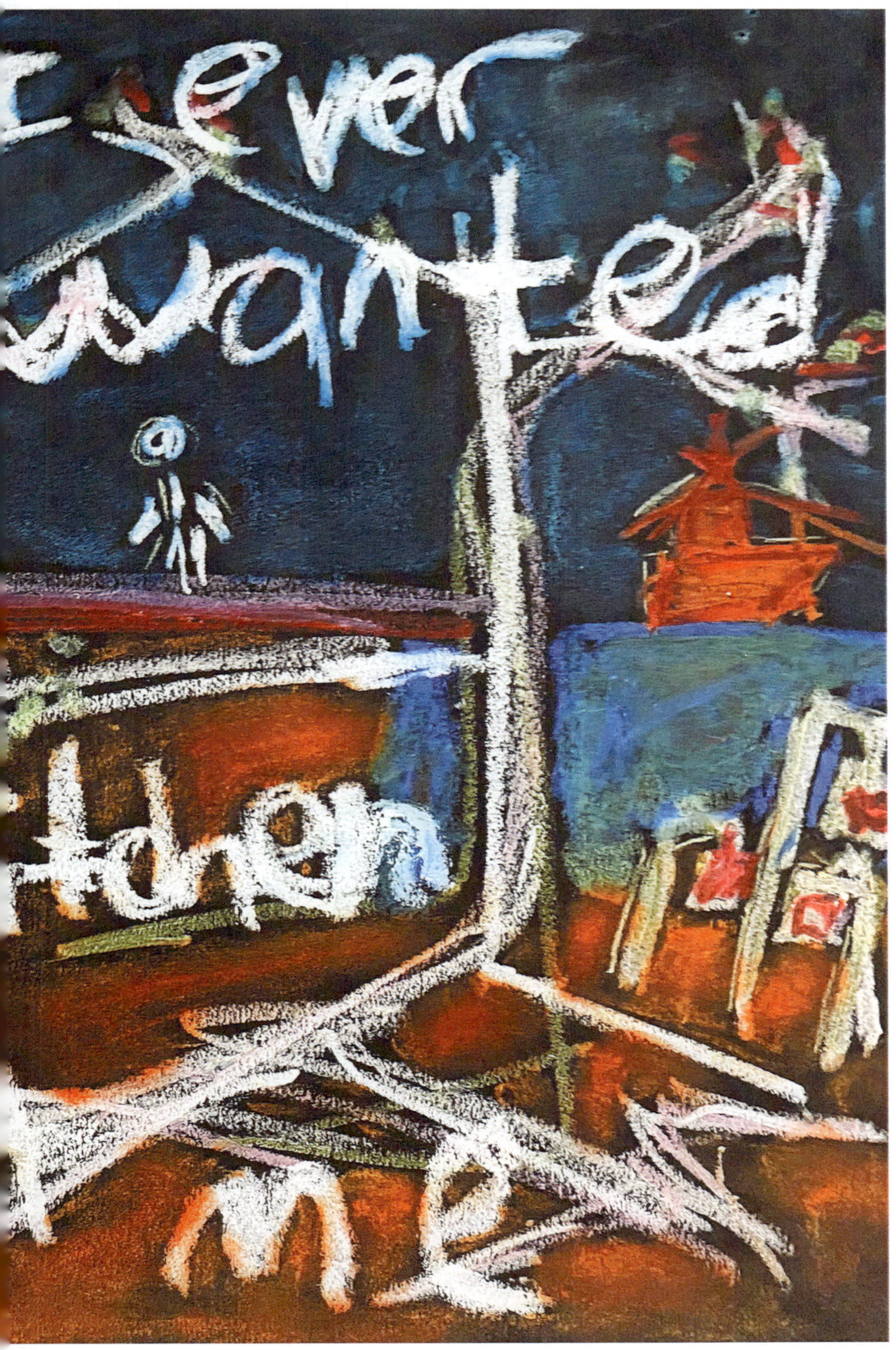

ever
wanted
me

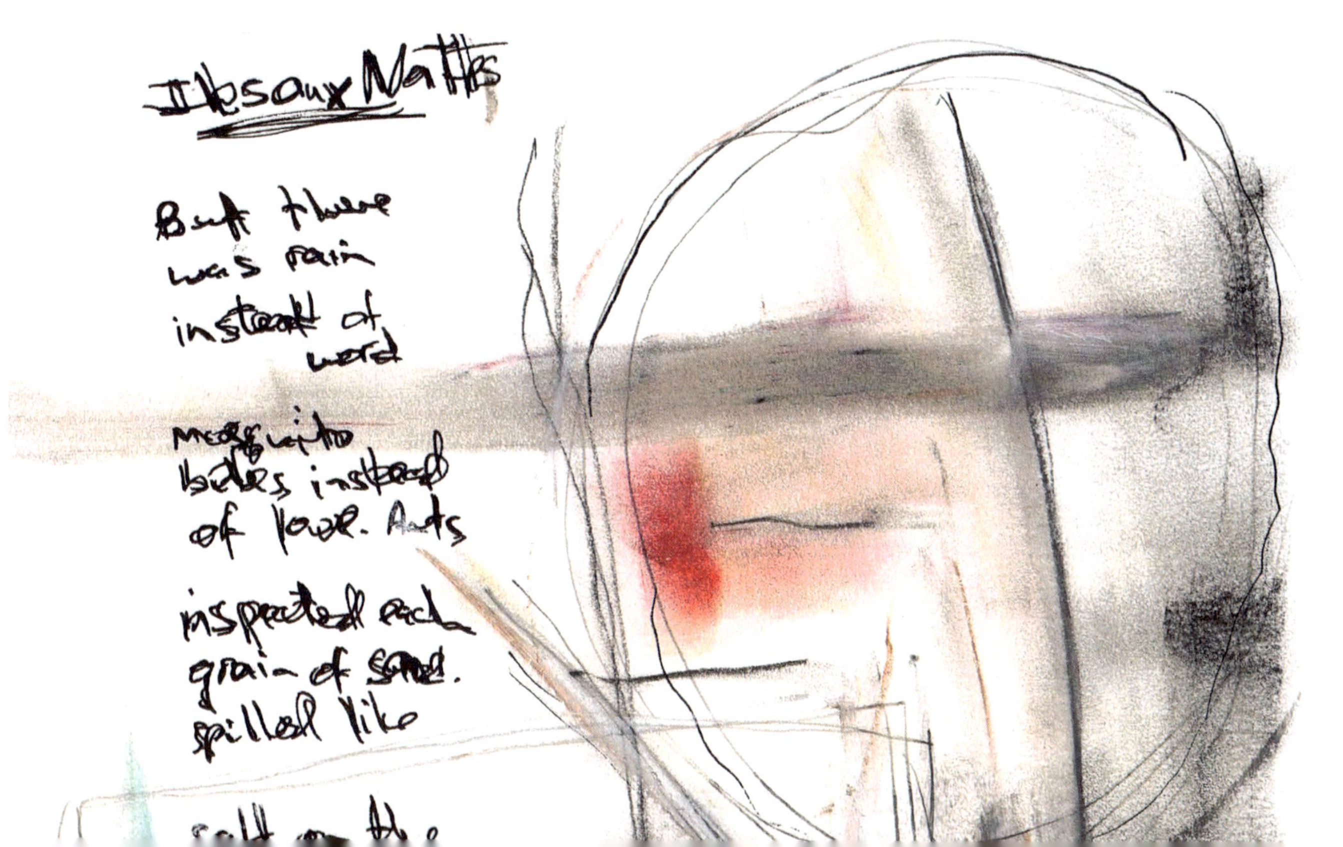
Illusory Moths
But there
was rain
instead of
word
mosquito
bites instead
of love. Ants
inspected each
grain of sand.
spilled like

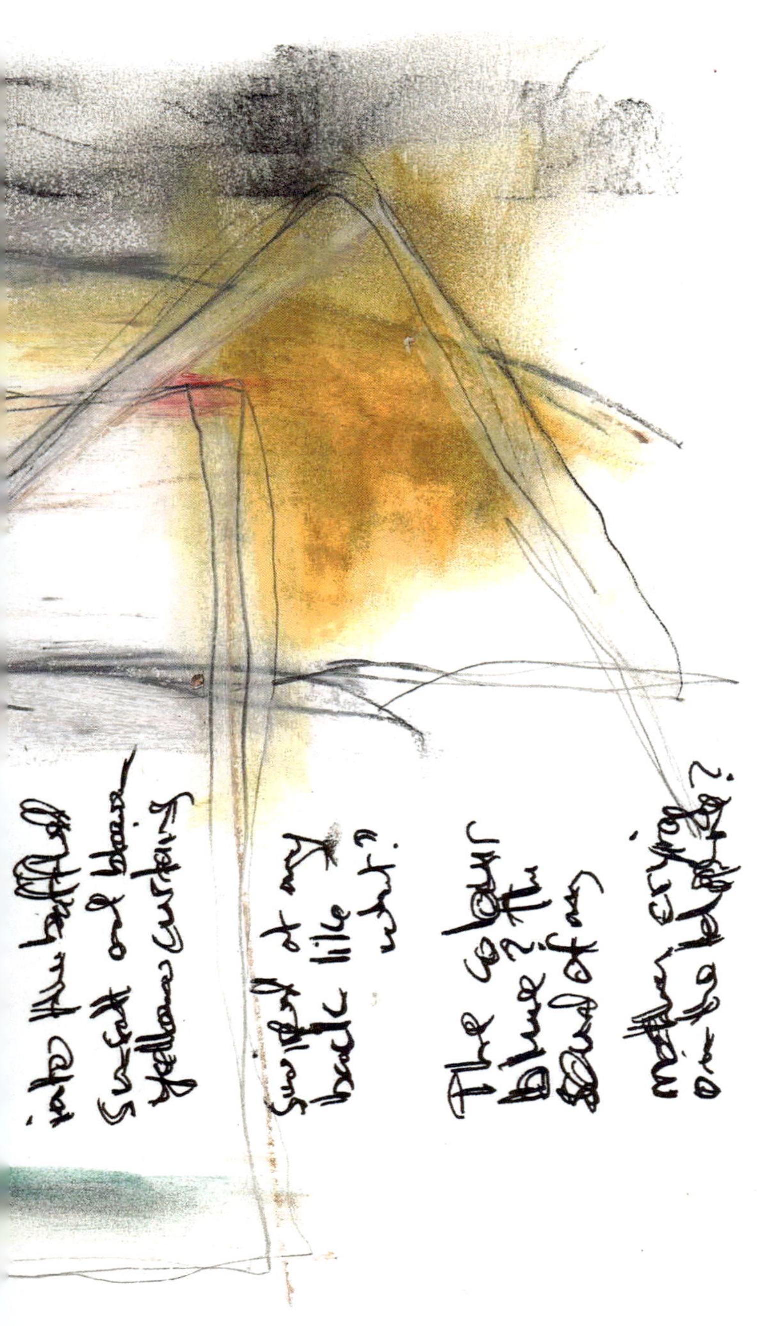

yellow curtains
back like
what?
The colour
blue? the
sound of my
mother crying

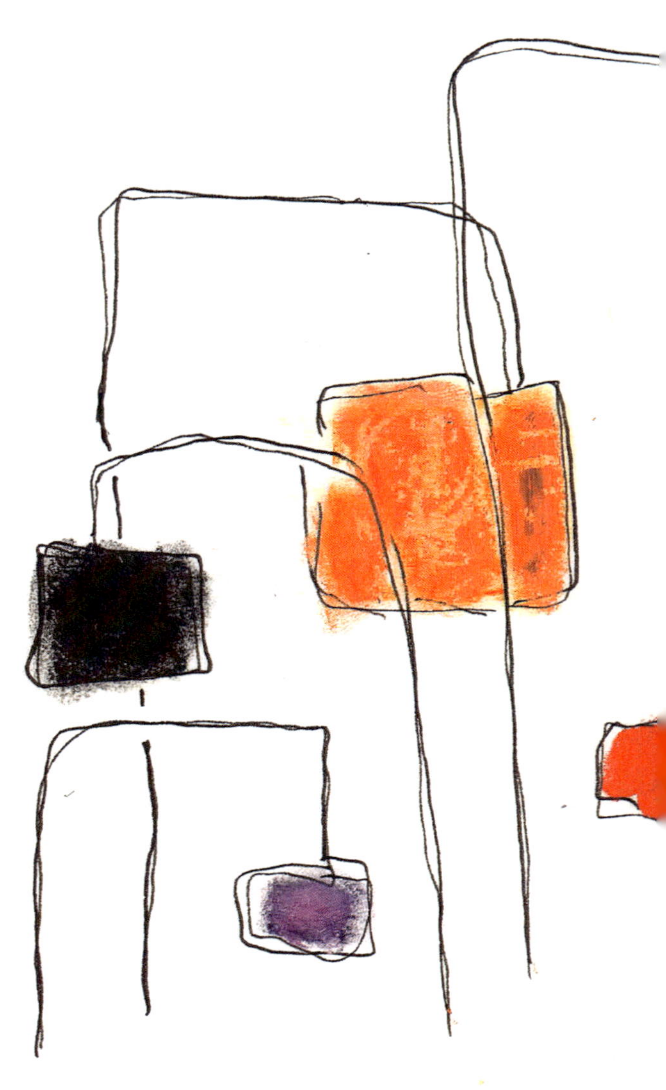

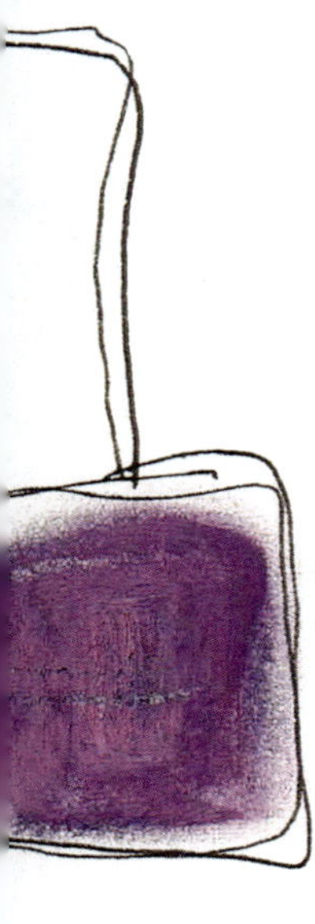

arriving home
to emptiness

try to keep busy

unpack

plan dinner

prepare the laundry

get through the list.

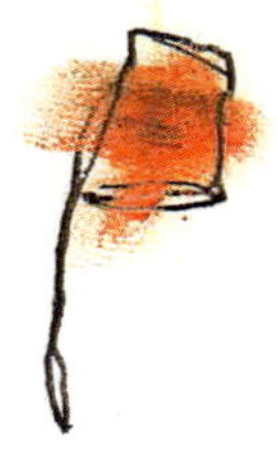

How much
can you get
used to

and still be
who you
were?

## Until you dig it out

The psychologists cannot replicate their findings,
smile as I might, I don't feel any happier. So

I seek out a change of scene to avoid the settling
gloom and now physics tells me that light has a
source.

It's tempting to believe that darkness does too.

Now Physics tells me that light has a source and it's tempting to believe that darkness does too.

So. I seek out a change of scene to avoid the settling gloom.

The psychologists cannot replicate their findings. Smile as I might, I don't feel any happier. Desparate. Desparate. Desparate. Desparate.

Desparate.

Desparate. Desparate. Desparate. Desparate.

How dark is the heart until you dig it out?

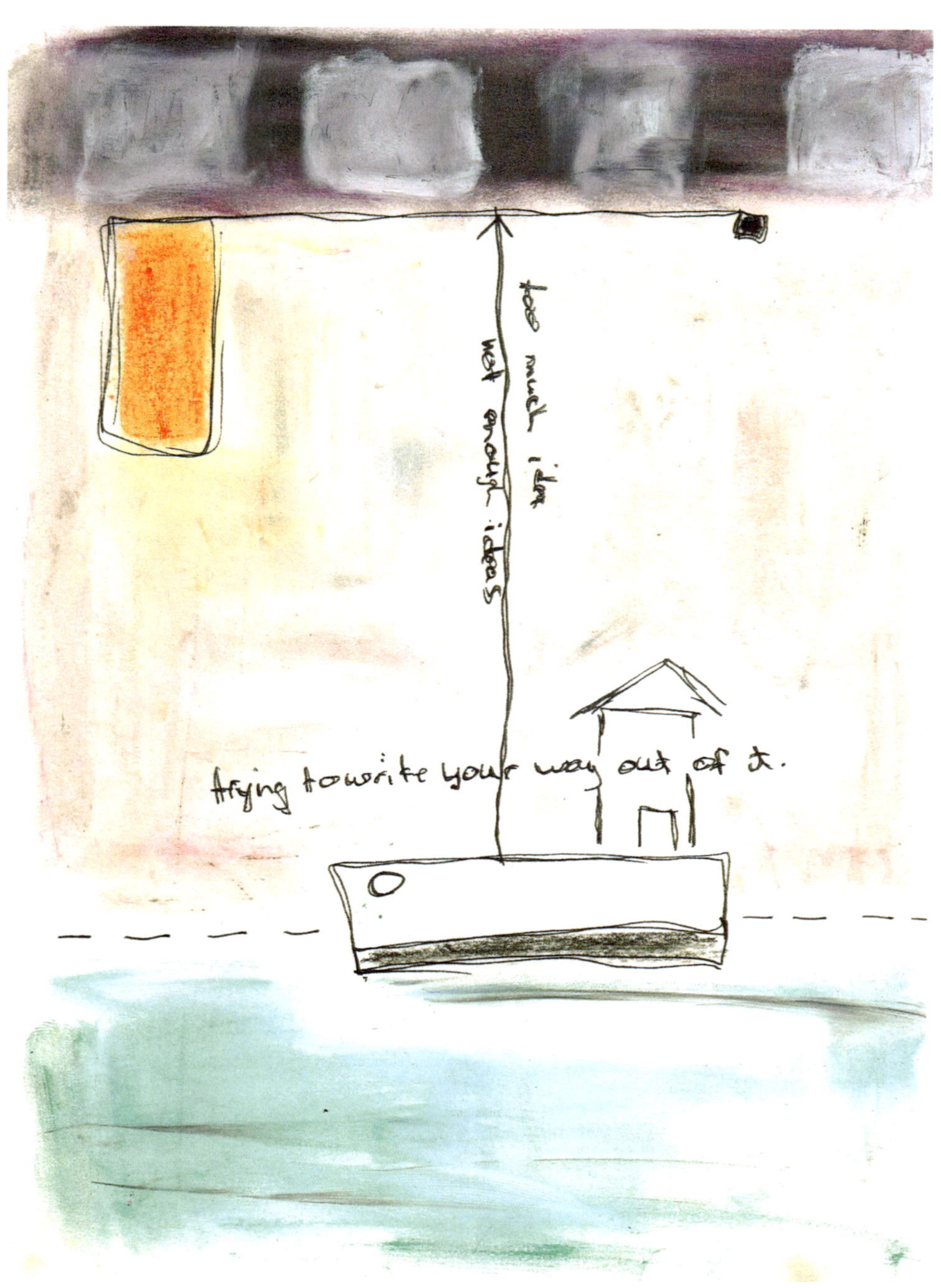
too much idea
not enough ideas
trying to write your way out of it.

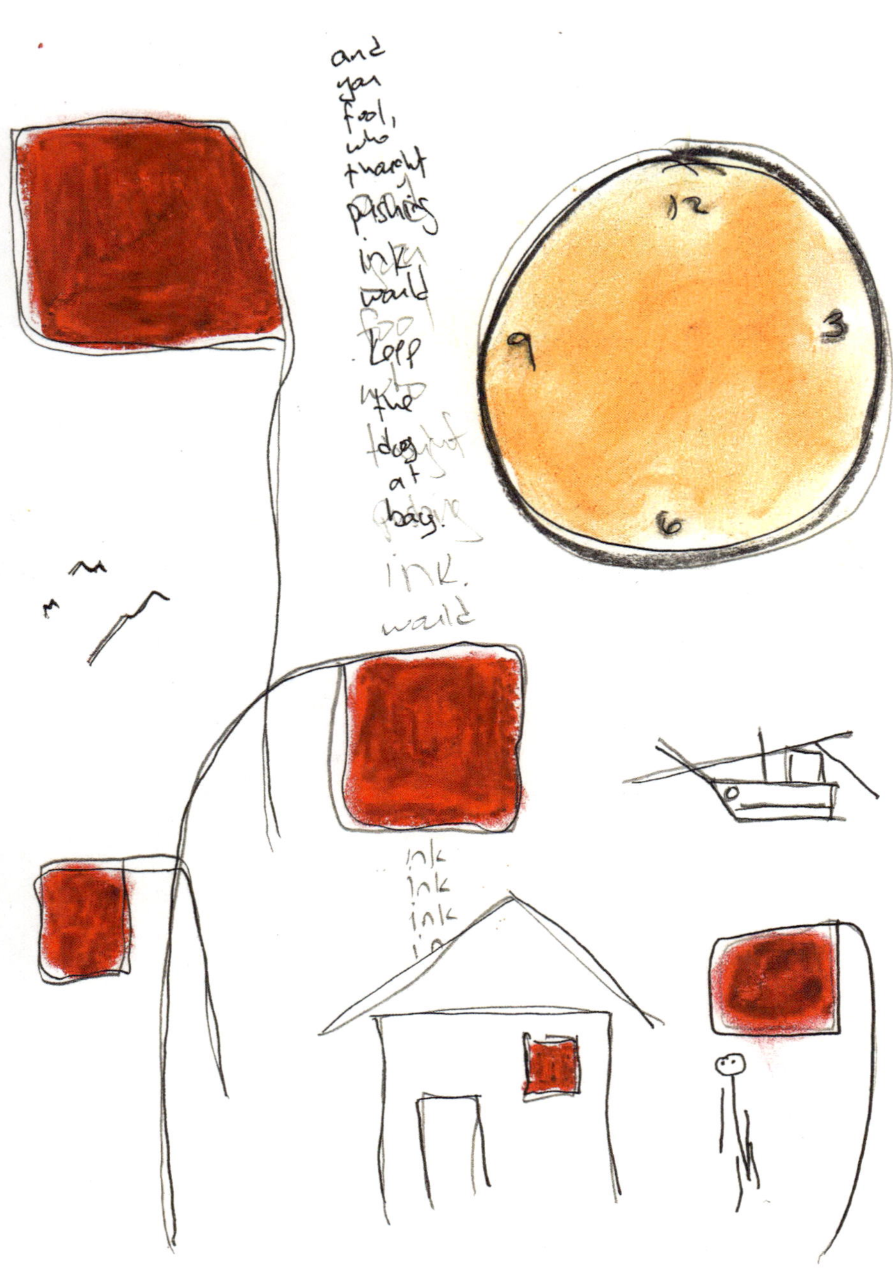
and
you
fool,
who
thought
polishing
ink
would
keep
the
dog
at
bay!
ink
would
12
3
6
9
ink
ink
ink

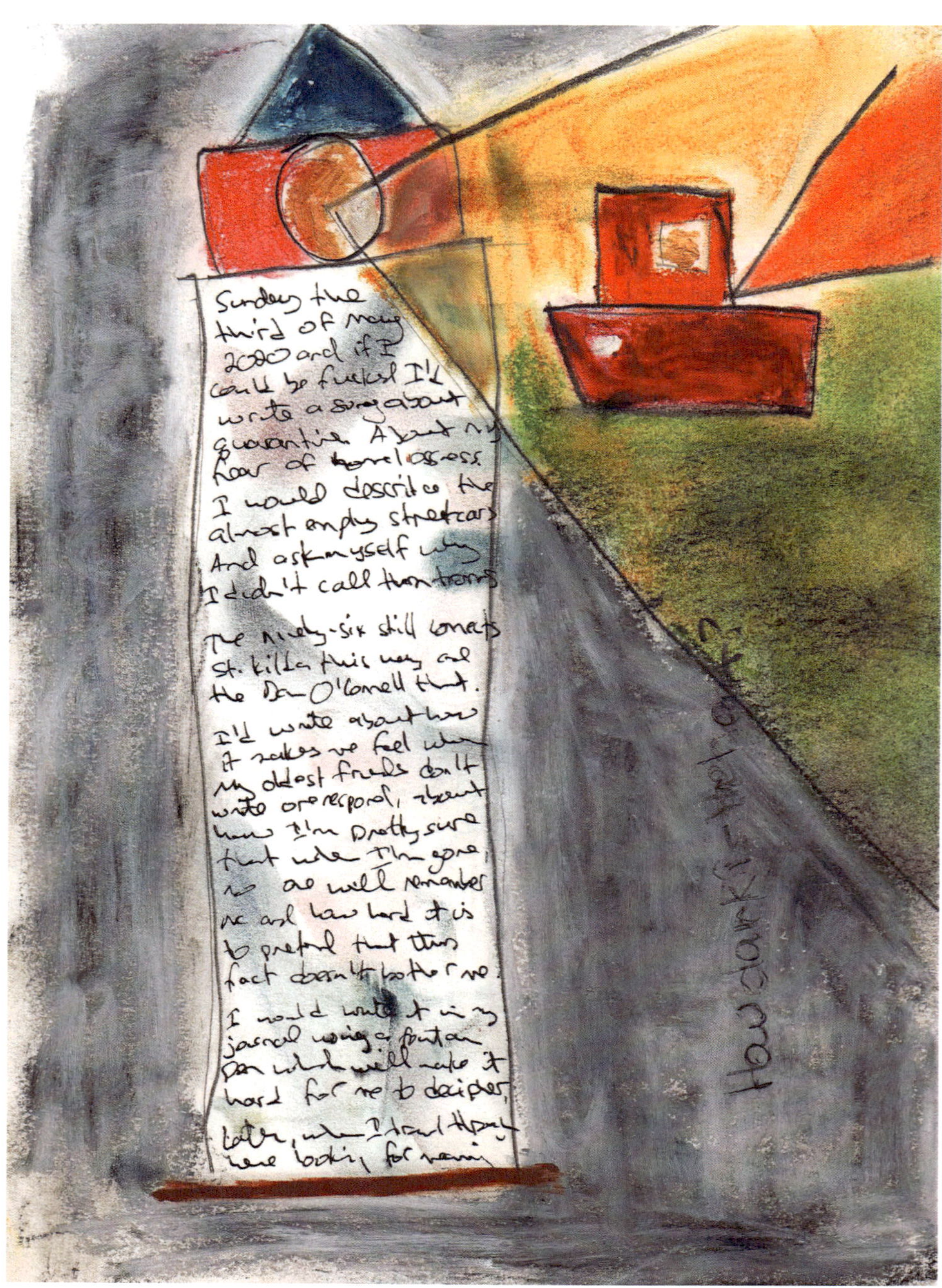

Sunday the
third of May
2020 and if I
could be fucked I'd
write a song about
quarantine. About my
fear of homelessness.
I would describe the
almost empty streetcars
And ask myself why
I didn't call them trams

The ninety-six still connects
St. Kilda this way and
the Dan O'Connell that.
I'd write about how
it makes me feel when
my oldest friends don't
write or respond, about
how I'm pretty sure
that when I'm gone,
no one will remember
me and how hard it is
to pretend that this
fact doesn't bother me.

I would write it in my
journal using a fountain
pen which will make it
hard for me to decipher,
later, when I trawl through
here looking for meaning
How dark is — that?

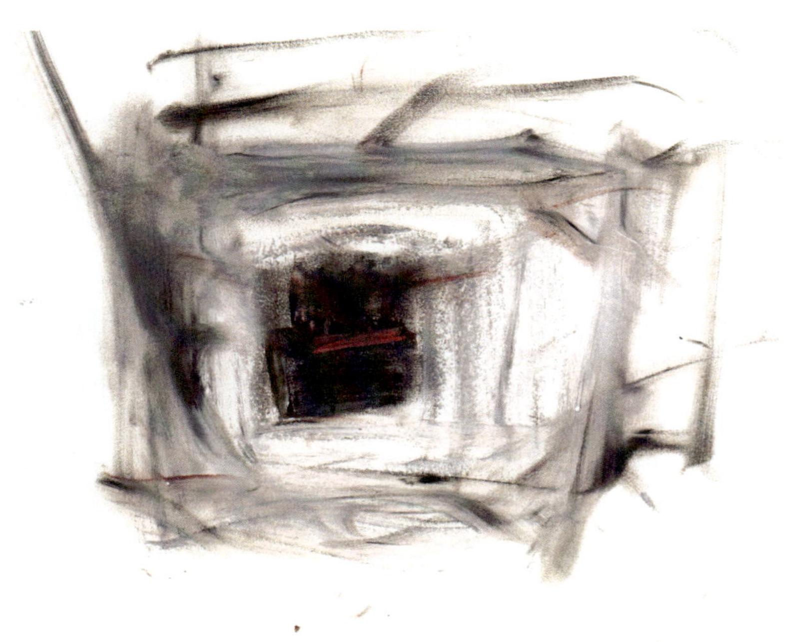

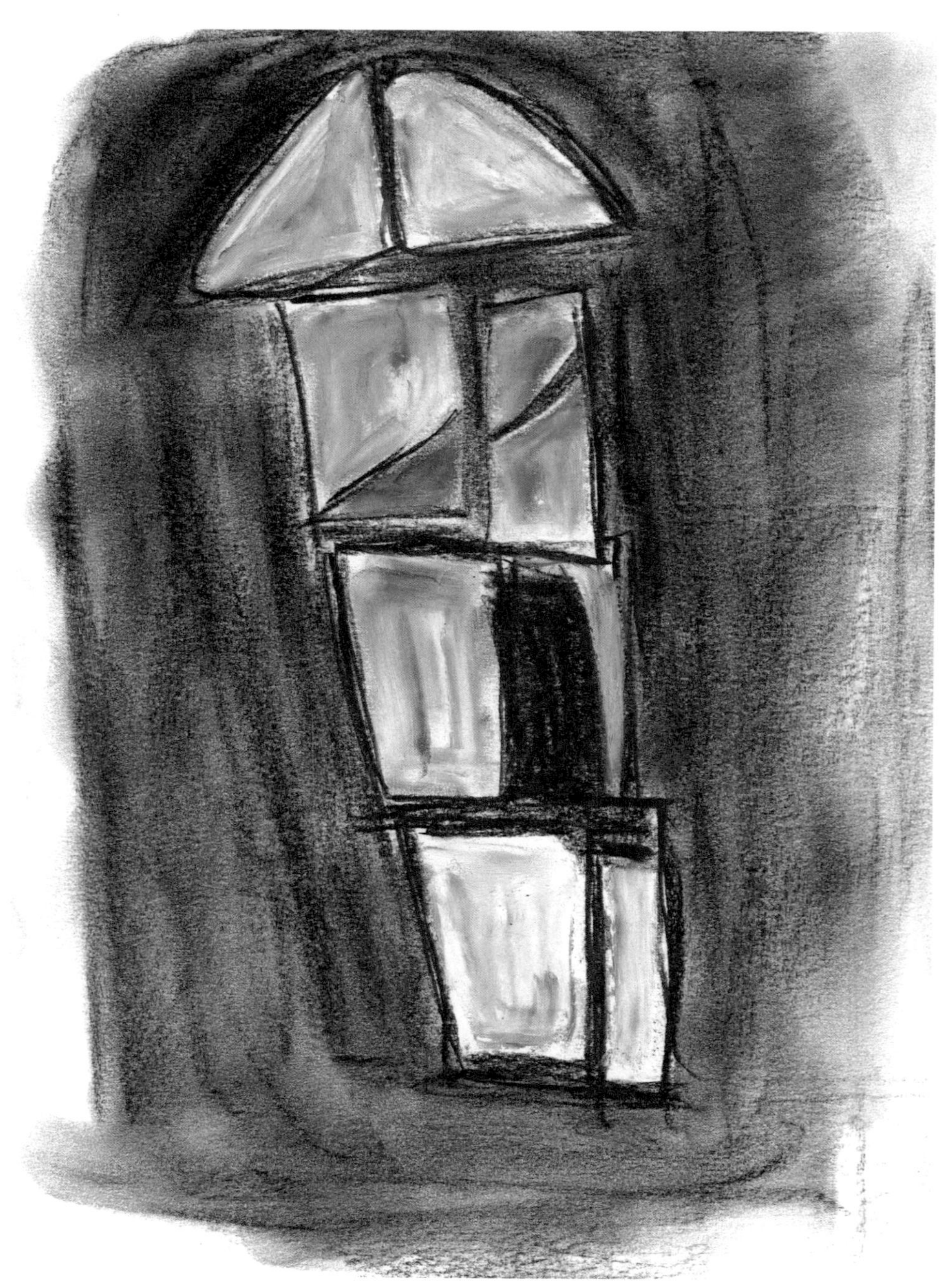

## Scraps and missed directions.

To imagine a life as fiction
supposes somebody

could to take the time
to make you up.

A lifetime, begging
for some kind of frame

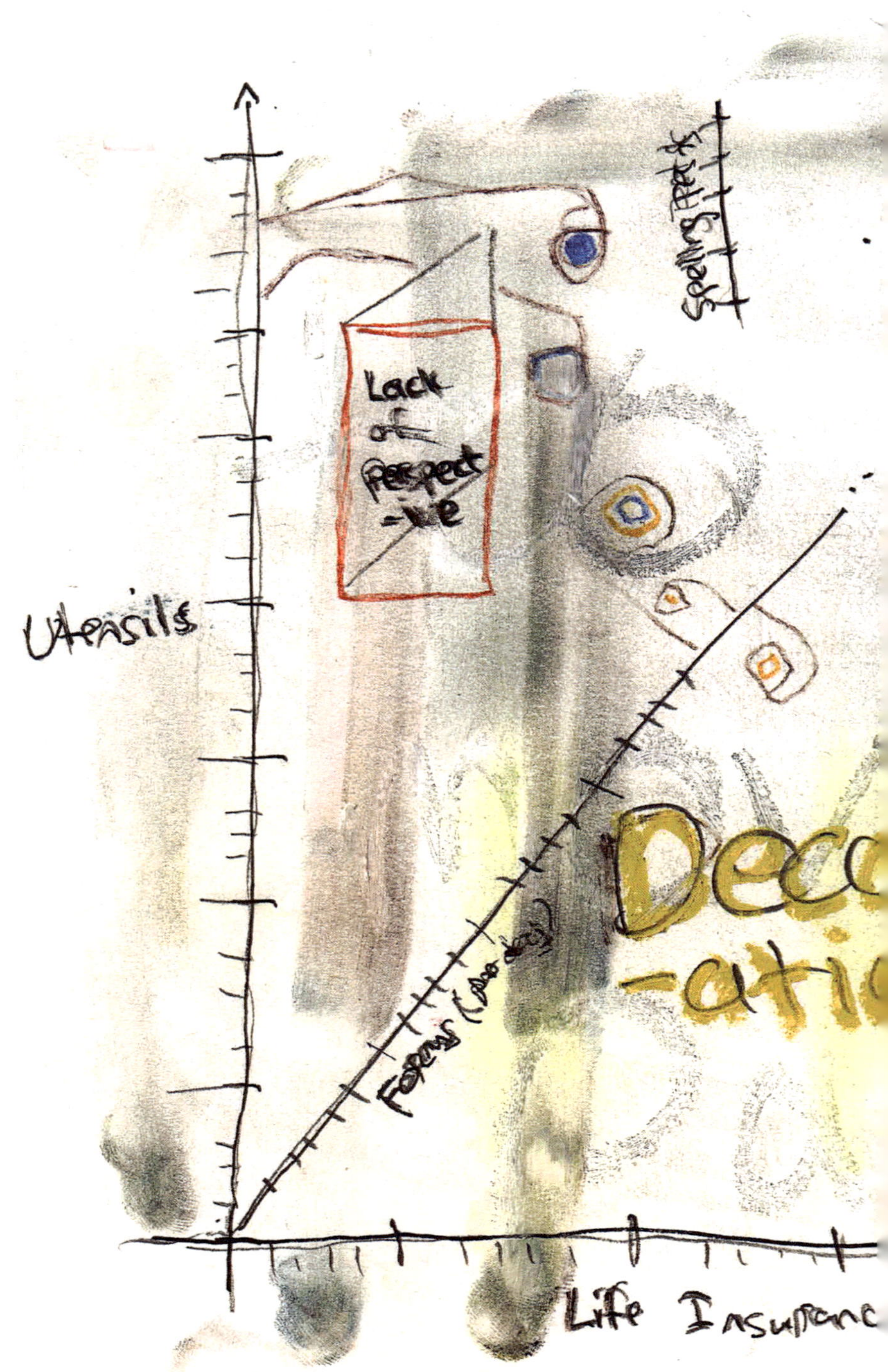
Utensils
Lack of Respect -ive
Spelling Pets
Forms (also docs)
Deco -atio
Life Insuranc

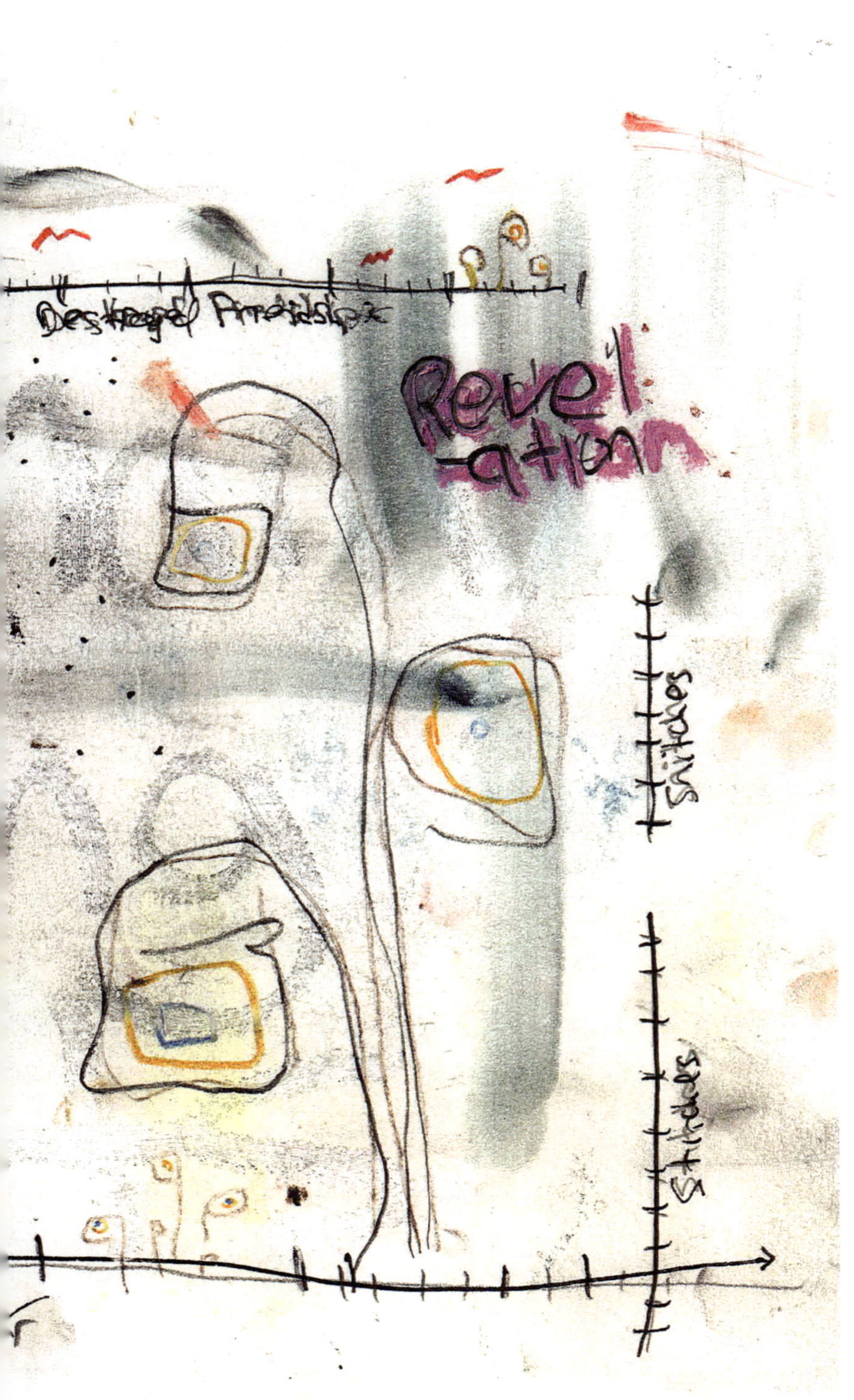
Revel
-ation
Snitches
Stitches

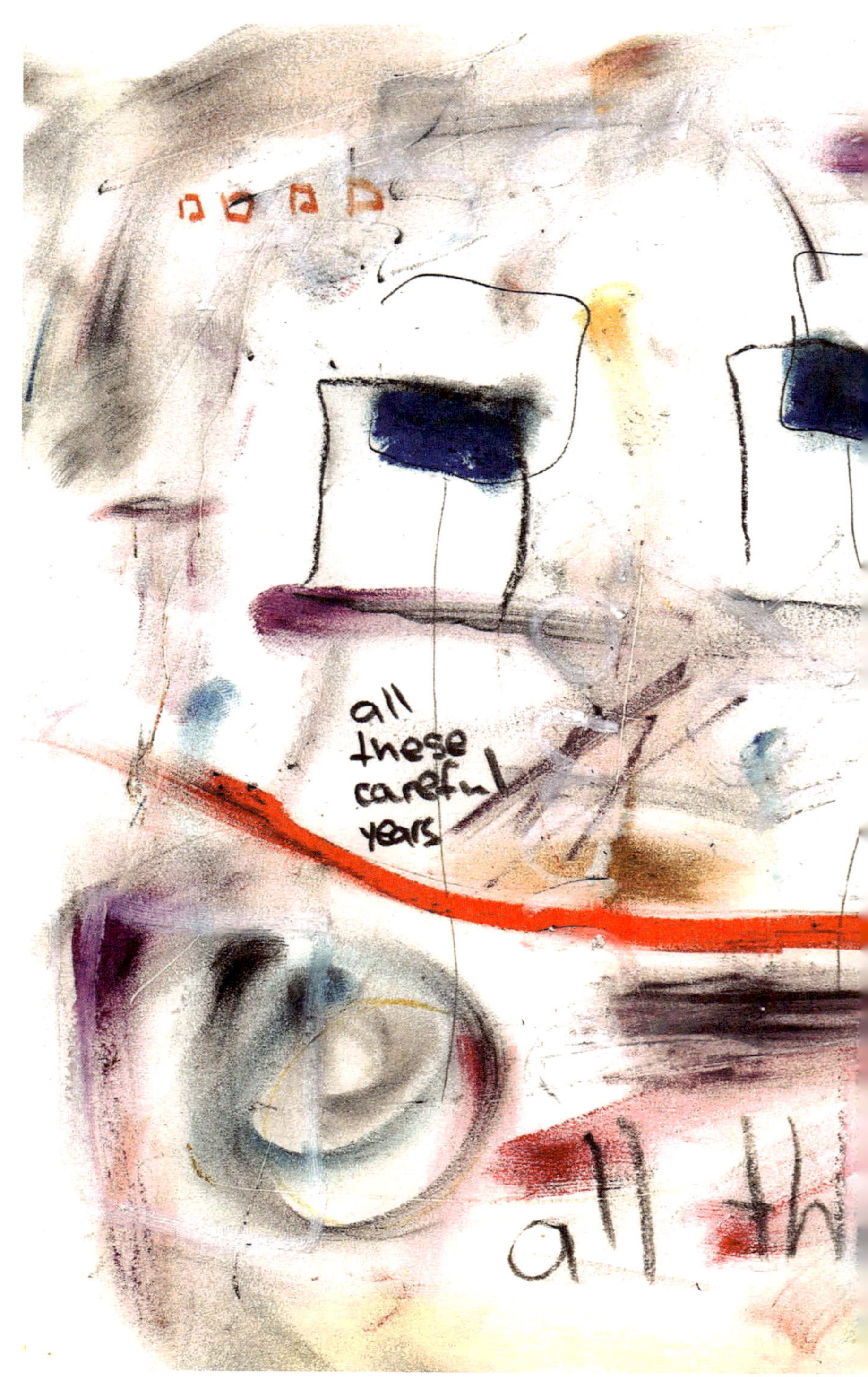
all these careful years
all th

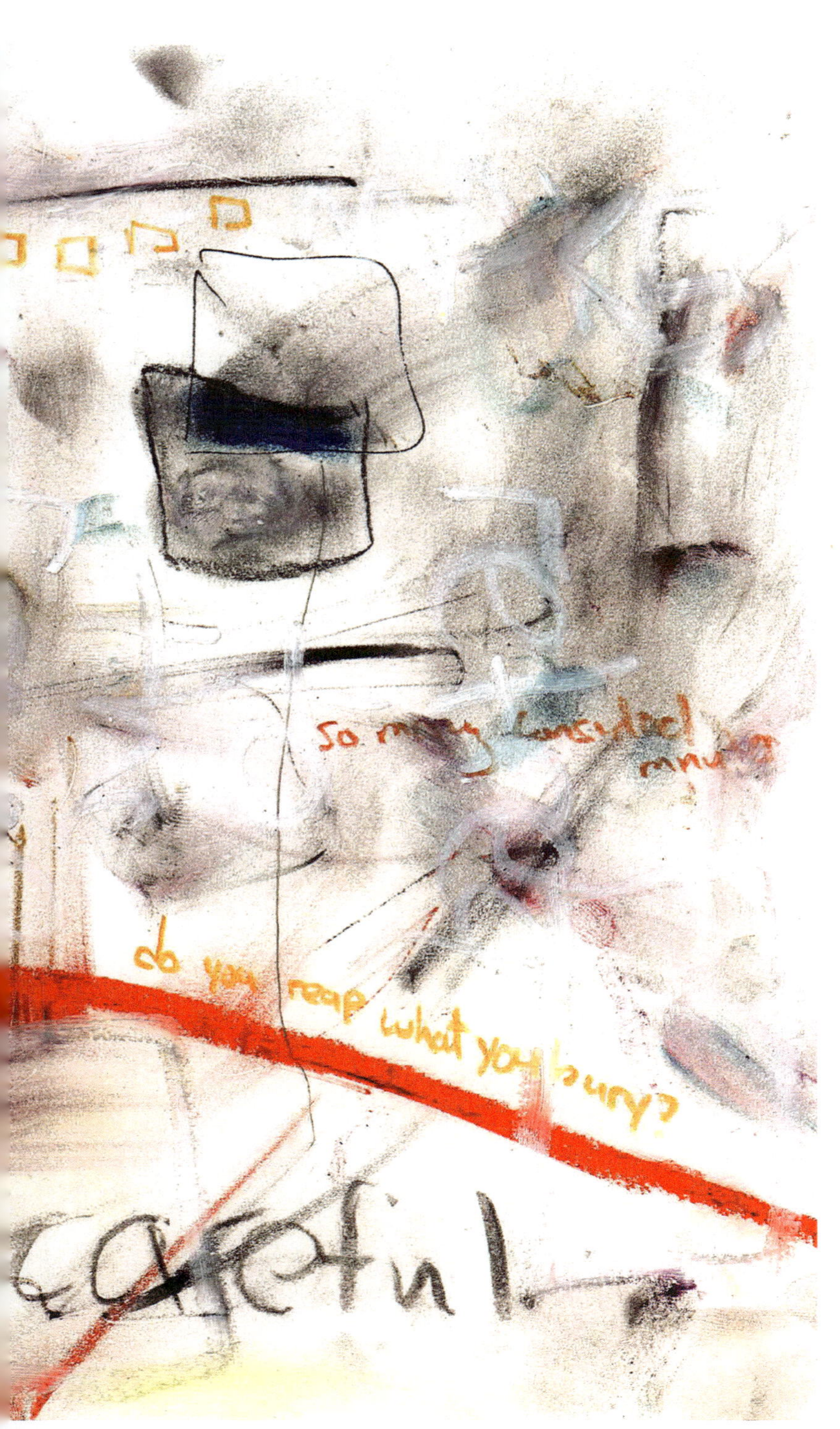
do you reap what you bury?
careful

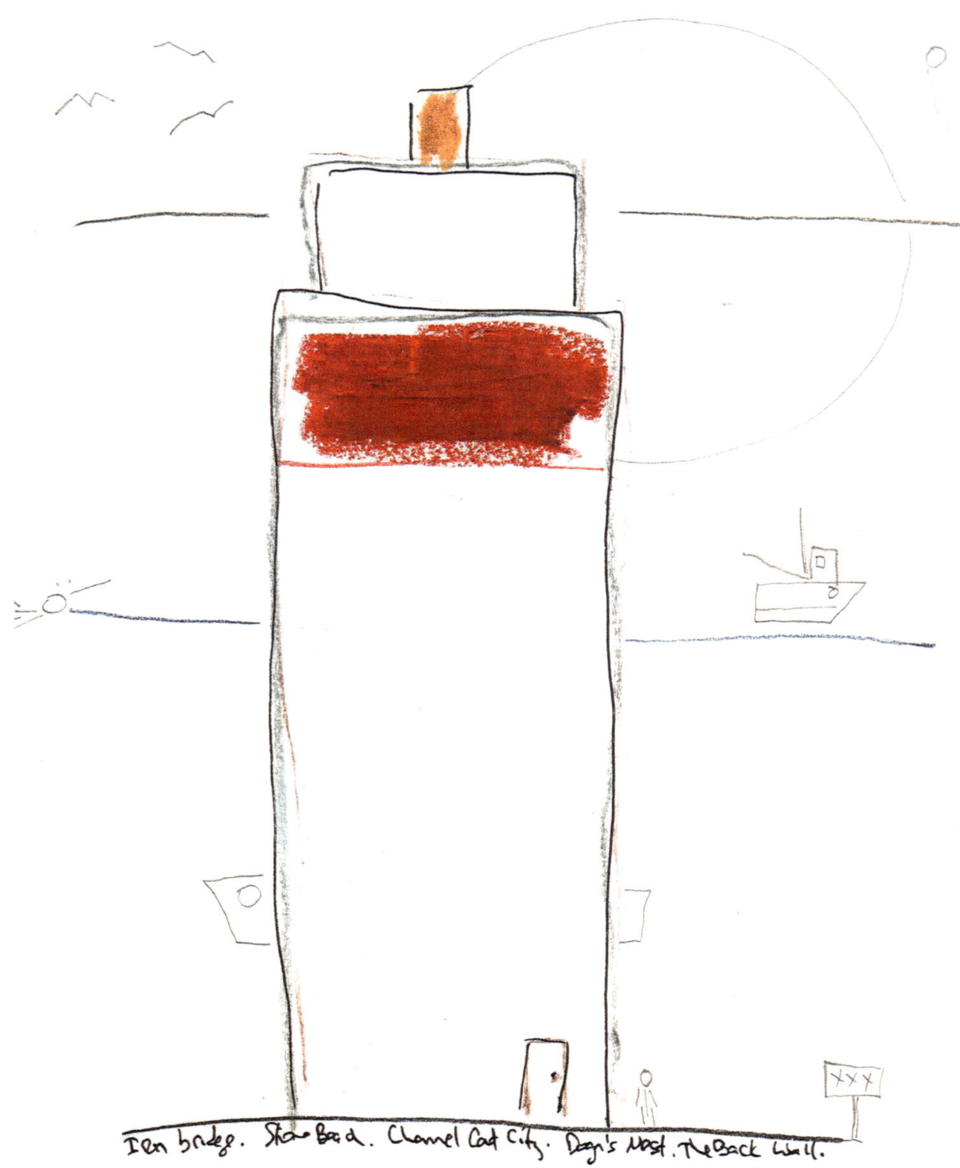
XXX
Iron bridge. Stone Beach. Channel Cat City. Dog's Nest. The Back Wall.

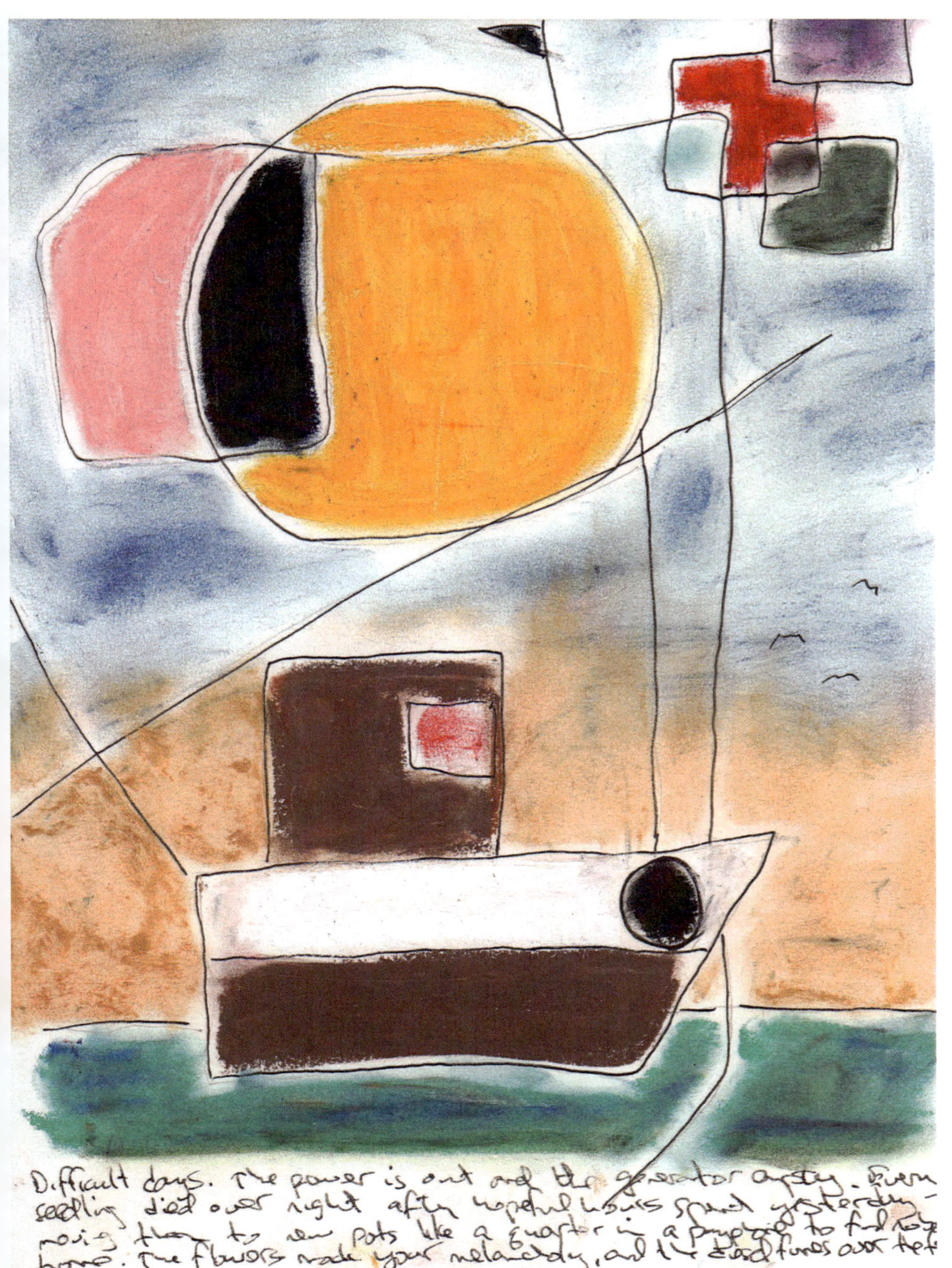
Difficult days. The power is out and the generator empty. Every
seedling died over night after hopeful hours spent yesterday -
moving them to new pots like a quarter in a
home. The flowers made your melancholy, and the dead fumes over

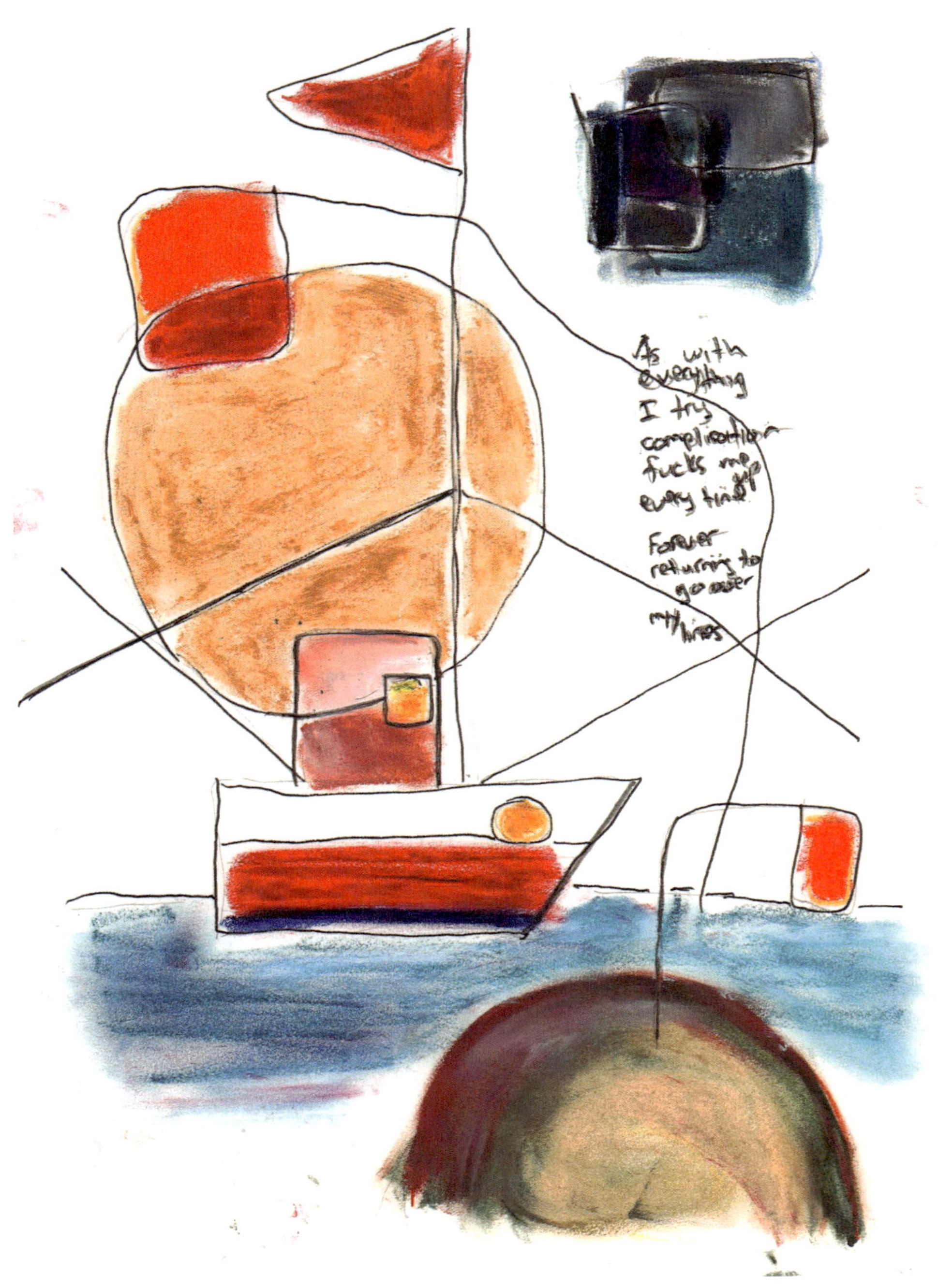
As with
everything
I try
complication
fucks me up
every time
Forever
returning to
go over
my lines

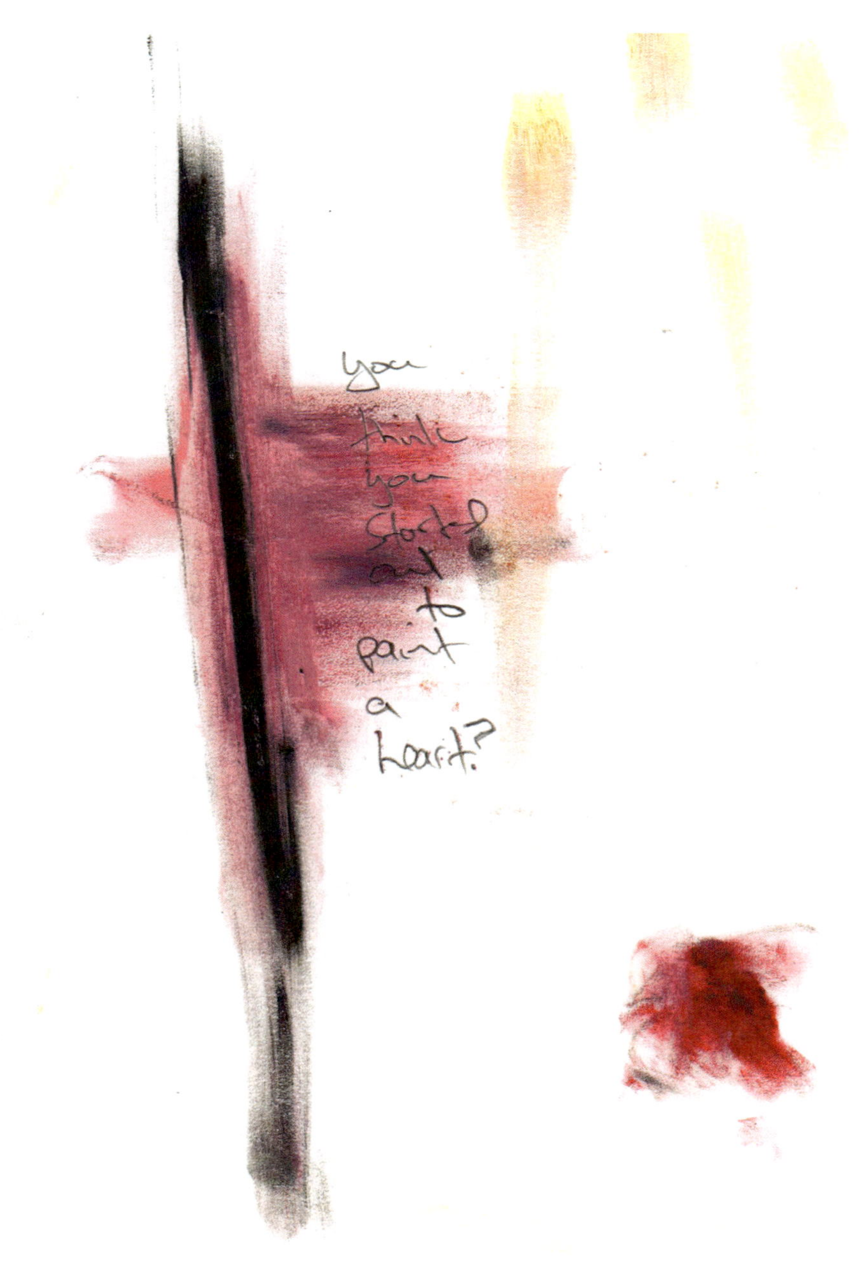
you
think
you
started
out
to
paint
a
heart?

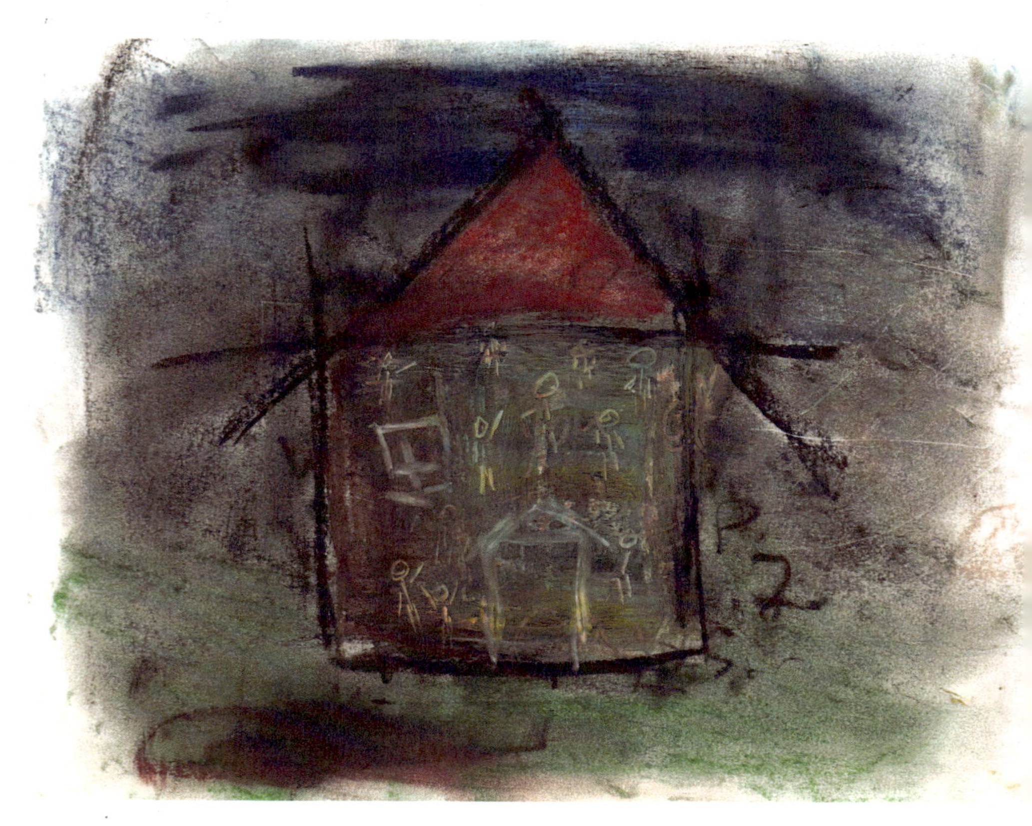

## In So Many Words

The hammock slung across the front of the pergola, a colourful smirk presented to the garden, the cracked cement lane and the rusty gate. Soon the guard who inhabits the shed at the back of the house will drag a hose out here and water the flowers and bushes and so on.

Each one of them has a name, I suppose, a way to call them, but I'll never sort them out in English let alone Latin, French or Malagasy Vines, creepers and suckers. A cactus that looks like a collection of beaver tails arranged in one vase and a sort of bereft Christmas tree in another.

Green, red, yellow, purple— you name it. The sky is dark blue now in the early evening, a complement to the light blue of the hammock. Would CMYK values have made this more real? Does the verb tense and the low word count offer enough resolution?

**Fred Biggar** has written and drawn a number of lines, made a few pictures and taught one good lesson.

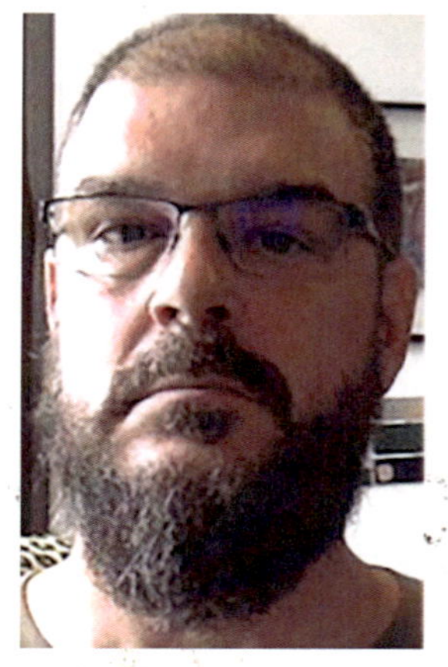

He is an alumnus of UBC's graduate creative writing program and holds a BA in Film and Communications from McGill University.

A Canadian, Fred is a permanent resident of Australia. He lives in Malaysia and Italy.

Enquiries: **mudroad@protonmail.com**

www.ingramcontent.com/pod-product-compliance
Lightning Source LLC
Chambersburg PA
CBRC091250050726
47599CB00013B/1044

* 9 7 8 1 7 6 3 6 8 1 4 0 8 *